THE LIBRARY OF AMERICAN LIVES AND TIMES™

COUNT CASIMIR PULASKI

From Poland to America, a Hero's Fight for Liberty

AnnMarie Francis Kajencki

The Rosen Publishing Group's
PowerPlus Books™
New York

For My Father, Francis Casimir Kajencki,
Military Historian and Member of the Greatest Generation

Published in 2005 by The Rosen Publishing Group, Inc.
29 East 21st Street, New York, NY 10010

First Edition

Editor's Note: All quotations have been reproduced as they appeared in the letters and diaries from which they were borrowed. No correction was made to the inconsistent spelling that was common in that time period.

Library of Congress Cataloging-in-Publication Data

Kajencki, AnnMarie Francis
     Count Casimir Pulaski: from Poland to America, a hero's fight for liberty/ AnnMarie Francis Kajencki.
          v.cm. — (The library of American lives and times)
     Includes bibliographical references and indexes.
     Contents: The Confederation of Bar — Background to the American Revolution — The Count comes to America — Commander of the Horse — Preparing the troopers for battle — The Pulaski Legion — Betrayal at Little Egg harbor — The cavalry defends Charleston, South Carolina — The Siege of Savannah — A hero's legacy — Timeline.
     ISBN 1-4042-2646-x (lib bdg.)
     1. Pulaski, Kazimierz, 1747—1779 — Juvenile literature. 2. Generals — United States — Biography — Juvenile literature. 3. United States. Army — Biography — Juvenile literature. 4. United States — History — Revolution, 1775—1783 — Cavalry Operations — Juvenile Literature. 5. United States — History — Revolution, 1775 — 1783 — Participation, Polish — Juvenile literature. 6. Poles — United States — Biography — Juvenile Literature. [1. Pulaski, Casimir, 1747—1779. 2. Generals. 3. United States — History — Revolution, 1775—1783.] I. Title. II. Series.

E207.P8K347 2005
973.3'46-dc21
[B]

                                                               2003010719
Manufactured in the United States of America

CONTENTS

Introduction

Know that as I could not submit to stoop before the sovereigns of Europe, so I came to hazard all for the freedom of America

—Count Casimir Pulaski
from an August 19, 1779, letter to
the Continental Congress

Count Casimir Pulaski, a Polish nobleman, joined the American fight for independence from Britain in 1777. In his homeland, Pulaski had fought to free Poland from Russian domination from 1768 until 1772. Although Poland was governed by the Polish king Stanislaw II August Poniatowski, the empress Catherine II of Russia controlled the king and most of the Polish nobility. To ensure Russia's domination of Poland, she stationed Russian soldiers on Polish soil. Casimir Pulaski led a small army of freedom fighters against the Russians.

Opposite: Julian Rys painted this portrait of Count Casimir Pulaski around 1897. When a soldier who had once served under Count Casimir Pulaski was asked about his former commander, the soldier replied, "He was a young and noble gentleman, a very daring horse-man, [who] feared nothing in the world."

Most of the Polish nobles, fearing the loss of their large estates, remained neutral. Pulaski's soldiers were finally overwhelmed by the superior strength of the enemy, and Pulaski was forced to flee the country to avoid capture.

After wandering around Europe for several years, Pulaski eventually ended up in France. There he learned of the American battle for independence. Pulaski wanted to help the Americans. He met with Benjamin Franklin and Silas Deane, the two American commissioners in Paris, who had come to France to gain support for the American cause.

Franklin knew little about the young Pole and hesitated to introduce Pulaski to American officials. The commissioners were also overwhelmed by requests from numerous foreign volunteers who sought promotion and glory in America. However, Pulaski's friends in France informed the two commissioners of Pulaski's military experience and his dedication to liberty. As a result, both Franklin and Deane wrote favorable letters of introduction to General George Washington, the commander in chief of America's Continental army.

Washington met with Casimir Pulaski after Pulaski had journeyed to America. Convinced of Pulaski's ability, Washington later recommended the count to Congress for an appointment as the first cavalry commander of the Continental army.

Pulaski served as a brigadier general from September 1777 to October 1779. A skilled horseman and soldier,

This 1917 poster, by W. T. Benda, of Thaddeus Kosciuszko (*left*) and Casimir Pulaski (*right*) urged men to join the army. The poster was captioned, "Poles! Kosciuszko and Pulaski fought for the liberty of Poland and other nations—follow their example—Enlist in the Polish Army!"

Pulaski trained the American cavalry to fight as an effective combat force. Later, Congress granted Pulaski permission to organize his own unit of horsemen and foot soldiers, which would become known as the Pulaski Legion. Throughout his service in America, Casimir Pulaski would prove his commitment to the cause of American freedom.

1. The Confederation of Bar

Jozef and Marianna Pulaski welcomed the birth of their second child on March 6, 1745. Devout Catholic parents normally waited two to three weeks before baptizing their newborn babies. However, as their baby seemed ill, Jozef and Marianna wanted the infant baptized immediately. Jozef sent for a priest, who rushed through the snow along the icy streets of Warsaw, the capital of Poland, to the Pulaski home and administered the sacrament of baptism. One week later, family and friends, many from families of royal lineage, gathered at the Holy Cross Church in Warsaw to participate in the formal baptismal ceremony for the baby Pulaski.

A common and old custom among the upper class was to provide multiple names for the child. Church records list four names for the newest Pulaski son: Kazimierz, Michal, Wladyslaw, and Wiktor. In all the records, Kazimierz appears first on the list. In a grand ceremony, the healthy baby son was christened Kazimierz. Later Kazimierz would be most widely known by the Anglicized form of his name, Casimir. The baby inherited the title of count from his father, who was granted the title by an earlier king.

For more than two and one-half centuries, books, encyclopedias, articles, and biographies have incorrectly identified the actual date and year of Casimir Pulaski's birth. The correct date of Pulaski's birth, March 6, 1745, was verified in August 1995, from records found in the archives of the Holy Cross Parish in Warsaw. Additionally, Casimir Pulaski was born in the family's Warsaw home, not in the Pulaskis' country estate of Winiary, located to the south of Warsaw.

Count Jozef Pulaski, shown in a painting from the 1700s, was appointed by the king to serve as Warka's *starosta*, or town official.

Casimir descended from a long line of Polish heroes. His forefathers had ridden in the Polish cavalry, a group of soldiers who rode and fought on horseback, under King Jan III Sobieski. In 1683, at the Siege of Vienna, Sobieski freed Europe from the Ottoman Turks who had raided Europe and advanced into the lands between France and Poland. At Vienna, King Sobieski led an allied army that defeated the Turks and saved the Holy Roman Empire.

Casimir's father, Jozef, was a wealthy and respected member of the gentry, or people of high social position, and a renowned lawyer. The public respected him because his conduct was honorable, fair, and above corruption.

Jozef placed the needs of his country above all others, unlike many other nobles, who tended their own needs first. Casimir's mother, Marianna, was from the wealthy Zielinski family. Casimir had an older brother, Franciszek, a younger brother, Antoni, and five younger sisters: Anna, Jozefa, Joanna, Paulina, and Malgorzata. The Pulaski family formed a close-knit group. The Pulaski children had governesses and were educated by tutors at home. The boys also received elementary training at the parish school in Warka, near the Pulaski estate, and later at a school in Warsaw where they were taught by Catholic priests.

Bernardo Bellotto depicted daily life in the Krakowskie Przedmiescie, a type of plaza, in Warsaw, Poland, in 1778. The Holy Cross Church, where Count Casimir Pulaski was formally baptized, is on the left side of the painting.

Jozef wanted to further his son's education, so he sent the fifteen-year-old Casimir to the court of Prince Karl, the son of Poland's King Augustus III. Noblemen often sent their sons to the royal courts. Prince Karl's court was located far away from Warsaw in an area called Courland in the city of Mitawa, which is in present-day Latvia.

During his stay at the court, Casimir observed the actions of Russian diplomats who were also present at the court. Casimir witnessed the many schemes the Russians used to weaken the autonomy of Poland, such as stationing Russian soldiers in Courland and restricting the actions of the prince. Casimir's experience in the court made him want to protect Poland. For centuries Russian czars had tried to take over Poland, and Catherine II, the empress of Russia from 1762 to 1796, continued this quest.

All across Europe in the eighteenth century, militarism grew at an enormous rate. The ideals of the military profession were emphasized, and the strength of the military determined government policies. Austria, Prussia, and Russia were the three dominant powers in Europe. Russia, in particular, continued to invade Poland. While other European countries increased their armed forces, Poland began neglecting its army. The country was weary from centuries of protecting its borders from foreign invaders such as the Russians, the Turks, the Tartars, and the Swedes. What Poland needed in the eighteenth century was a strong king.

Bernardo Bellotto dramatized the 1764 election of King Stanislaw II August Poniatowski. Bellotto also went by the name of Canaletto the Younger, after his uncle, the artist Canaletto, with whom Bellotto had studied. In 1767, King Poniatowski invited Bellotto to reside in Poland as Poniatowski's court painter.

Long before, however, in 1572, the reigning king of Poland had died without an heir, and the nobles seized the chance to make the kingship elective and subject to the will of the nobles. The nobles limited the size of the national army for fear it would be used against them. They took great delight in their freedom from royal interference. At the same time, though, these changes resulted in a weak national state of which the Russians took advantage. Other European monarchs also took sides in the periodic elections, to promote their own candidates for king and to meddle in Poland's internal affairs.

At the election held in 1764, several competing groups of Polish magnates, or powerful, influential people, gathered just south of Warsaw in Mokotow for the purpose of casting their votes for a new king. Russia, Austria, and Prussia backed their own candidates as well. Empress Catherine II strongly supported the Polish noble Stanislaw August Poniatowski. To intimidate other candidates and their supporters, she ordered Russian army units to Warsaw. Poniatowski was elected. Catherine II influenced the new king through her personal representative in Poland, Nikolay Repnin. She also kept a large army in Poland, primarily to support the rule of King Poniatowski.

The erosion of Poland's power troubled Count Jozef Pulaski and other patriotic Polish magnates. Therefore, these men organized a patriotic movement of Polish gentry to oppose the ever-encroaching Russians. Casimir supported his father wholeheartedly. His brothers, Franciszek and Antoni, also stood with their father, as did brother-in-law Antoni Suffczynski,

Catherine II, shown in an eighteenth-century painting, halted King Poniatowski's 1766 attempt to reform the Polish government. The king had hoped to abolish the *liberum veto*, a crippling policy that required the unanimous consent of all the nobles before any law was passed.

The cavalry of the Confederation of Bar, shown in a watercolor, wore white leather belts across their chests and belts around their waists. Ammunition, guns, and swords were attached to these belts, thereby freeing a soldier's hands to guide his horse or attack the enemy.

husband of Casimir's sister Paulina. The Pulaski men traveled about the country, contacting like-minded gentry and laying the groundwork for the movement.

On February 29, 1768, Jozef Pulaski called an organizational meeting at a small town deep in the Polish Ukraine and near the border with Turkey. He selected the remote town of Bar to avoid attracting the attention of the king or the Russians. Because of this meeting place their group was called the Confederation of Bar. To connect the movement to Poland's Roman Catholic roots, and to give their cause added fervor, Jozef established the Military Order of the Knights of the Holy Cross. The first members were Jozef Pulaski and his three sons. Aside from the Military Order, the members of the Confederation voted to establish a military arm, a regiment of knights that would consist of thirteen troops of hussars and heavy cavalry, and six companies of light troops.

The hussars were horsemen who carried arms such as lances and swords. The heavy cavalry were also horsemen who carried swords and lances, but they carried pistols and wore armor as well. The light troops, or infantry, did not carry heavy equipment and could march rapidly. Jozef Pulaski, the leading force behind this movement, was chosen to command. His three sons and his son-in-law Antoni also led units in the regiment. It was not long before Casimir developed into a bold, imaginative leader and rose to command the entire military

This drawing was based on one of the original flags used by the Confederation of Bar. The Virgin Mary adorns the center of the flag. The Roman Catholic clergy supported the Confederation in its quest to liberate Poland.

Poland had long relied on its cavalry in battle. In 1683, King Jan III Sobieski led the Polish cavalry at the Siege of Vienna, where Poland and its allies defeated the Turks. Wojciech Kossak's modern painting, *Polish Hussars Parading in Front of King Jan III Sobieski,* depicts the inspection of the troops by the king.

force of the Confederation, which numbered at times as many as four thousand soldiers. The Confederation consisted of a civilian as well as a military division. The civilian division engaged in matters of diplomacy.

The Russians first ignored the Confederates, as members of the Confederation were called. Before the Russians became fully aware of the growing Confederation, Casimir and other leaders continued to travel about the country, visiting nobles, collecting supplies, and recruiting additional men. However, the activities of the Confederates began to worry Nikolay Repnin, Catherine II's representative in Poland.

Repnin ordered General Peter Krechetnikov to march with eight thousand soldiers against the Confederates. Around April 20, 1768, Casimir clashed with a detachment of Russian soldiers near the town of Staro-Konstantynow. The detachment was Krechetnikov's advance guard, and Casimir forced the Russians to retreat. An advance guard is the troops that are sent to explore a region before the main army arrives. Casimir Pulaski then withdrew to the town of Staro-Konstantynow and prepared to defend it.

On the morning of April 24, 1768, the Russians attacked the town with more than four thousand soldiers. The twenty-three-year-old Casimir defended his position with fewer than two thousand men. The Russians reported waging the attack for four hours without being able to defeat the Poles. Casimir said his smaller force successfully protected the town for more than ten hours. Because of Russian superiority, Casimir did not wait for the enemy to attack the next day. Under cover of darkness, he slipped away with his soldiers, the wounded, and the supplies to the neighboring town of Chmielnik.

The Russian commander, Podgorychanin, followed Casimir to Chmielnik. For three days the Russians attacked the Poles in five separate attacks, but all assaults were repulsed.

Meanwhile, Jozef Pulaski had initially been encouraged by the support of Prince Joachim Potocki, a powerful magnate who possessed a private army. Potocki allied himself with the Confederates. In his first encounter with the Russians, however, Potocki was careless in defending the town where his army rested. During the night the Russians attacked unexpectedly from all sides and destroyed Potocki's force in one engagement. This disaster severely damaged the Confederate cause. Other magnates who might have considered joining Jozef Pulaski became fearful and chose instead to remain neutral.

Casimir continued to lead the Confederate army and gained experience with each battle and skirmish. Although he lost some of his soldiers, he always managed to remove his unit from difficult entanglements. At the fortified monastery at Berdyczow, 5,000 Russian troops attacked Casimir's 1,400 soldiers. After a two-week siege, the Russians captured the monastery as well as Casimir and his garrison. The Russians then seized Bar, the birthplace of the Confederation. Jozef, his two sons, and about 2,000 Confederate soldiers managed to escape across the Dniester River into Turkey. After holding Casimir captive for one month, the Russians released him, and he joined his father in Turkey.

The Confederates of Bar soon reentered Poland and continued the struggle for three more years. The Confederation could not convince France or Turkey to help its cause, and other Polish magnates remained

Juliusz Fortunat Kossak's 1883 watercolor portrays Casimir Pulaski at the December 1770 Battle of Czestochowa. In the Polish town of Czestochowa, in September 1770, Pulaski and the army of the Confederation of Bar set up their base of operation. They defended their position from within the protective walls of the monastery Jasna Gora. That winter the Poles outlasted a Russian siege and a later attack, and maintained their hold on Czestochowa and the fortified monastery.

fearful of losing their vast lands. In desperation, a group of Confederates conceived a plot to abduct King Stanislaw II August Poniatowski and persuade him to turn against the Russians. They had no intention of harming the king and thought that he might be used to bargain with the enemy. The plan was risky. If a scheme to abduct the king failed, his captors would be executed. Casimir may have known of the plot, but he did not take part in the kidnapping.

On the evening of November 3, 1771, the plotters kidnapped the king from his carriage in Warsaw. As they led their prisoner out of the city, the Confederates became frightened of the consequences and worried that they were being pursued. They released the king and fled.

The best-known and feared Confederate, Casimir Pulaski, was blamed for the kidnapping and for attempted regicide, or the killing of a king, even though the ruler had been released unharmed. Casimir, who had not been captured, was tried in absentia, a Latin phrase meaning "in absence," and was condemned to death. Casimir Pulaski was forced to leave his homeland. If he stayed in Poland, he faced execution. Jozef, his father, died in a Turkish prison, and his brother Franciszek was killed in battle. After four years, the Confederation of Bar had collapsed.

Casimir would never return to Poland. He wandered around Europe for a number of months. In France, he fell into debt and was thrown into a debtor's prison. Friends, however, paid money for his release. When news reached France of the outbreak of the American Revolution, Pulaski's spirits were lifted. Perhaps he could bring honor to his own country if he fought for another nation in a noble cause.

Influential friends in France interceded on Casimir's behalf with the American commissioners Benjamin Franklin and Silas Deane. After meeting Casimir, both Franklin and Deane decided to write letters of recommendation to General George Washington. With these letters in hand, Pulaski sailed toward America to continue his life as a freedom fighter.

2. Background to the American Revolution

The people who settled the British colonies in North America were resourceful. Many had immigrated to America to escape religious persecution and oppression in Europe. Initially, however, they remained tied to the homeland from which they had come. When Americans faced the hostile French settlers in Canada and in the region of the Great Lakes, they looked to Britain for protection.

France and Britain had been enemies for centuries and they were often engaged in warfare with each other. In 1756, the two countries fought each other in the Seven Years' War in Europe. They waged war in North America, too, where the conflict was called the French and Indian War. The fighting in North America had begun earlier, in 1754, over territorial domination of the new continent. The fighting ended when Britain defeated France at the battles at Quebec in 1759 and Montreal in 1760. The war officially came to an end with the 1763 Treaty of Paris, in which France ceded to Britain most of its colonial land claims in North America.

A member of Parliament addresses his fellow representatives in the British House of Commons in Anton Hickel's painting from around 1766. After the French and Indian War, Parliament taxed Americans to pay off the debt from the war.

After the French were defeated, the Americans felt less dependent on the British government for protection. Parliament, however, believed that Americans should help to pay off the huge debt that had been acquired from fighting the French and passed a number of new taxes. Americans did not accept this reasoning, especially as they had no voice in deciding how these new taxes were to be imposed.

Colonial resentment would only increase over the coming years. In 1764, Parliament passed the Sugar Act,

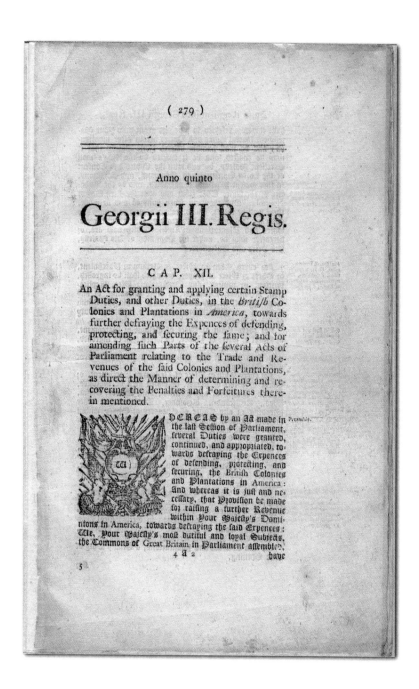

This guideline to the 1765 Stamp Act was printed in London in 1766, by Mark Baskett for King George III, whose name appears in Latin in the headline. The British wrote that the money raised from the tax will be used to defend the "British Colonies and Plantations in America."

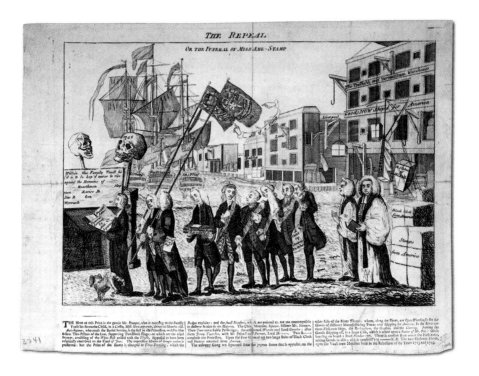

This 1766 cartoon expresses an artist's pleasure in the repeal of the hated British Stamp Act. The artist presents a funeral procession in which mourners walk toward the tomb of the Stamp Act. The fourth man from the left carries a coffin, marked with the birth and death dates of the act, 1765–1766.

which, along with a tax on imported molasses and sugar, sought to restrict American trade. In 1765, Parliament imposed the Quartering Act, forcing colonists to provide housing for British soldiers in America. That same year, the British government also passed the Stamp Act, which levied a tax through the purchase of a stamp that was to be attached to legal documents, books, insurance policies, newspapers, and playing cards.

Americans fiercely opposed the Stamp Act until Parliament finally repealed the act in 1766. Not long after, King George III appointed Charles Townshend as chancellor of the exchequer, a post similar to the U.S. secretary of the treasury. Townshend proposed additional strategies for raising funds, including the despised Townshend Acts of 1767, which called for a tax on imported paint, lead, paper, glass, and tea. In 1770, in reaction to an American boycott, or a refusal to buy these imported goods, Parliament repealed most of these taxes, except for a small tax on tea.

One night in December 1773, a group of Americans disguised as Mohawk Indians boarded British merchant ships that were docked in Boston Harbor and dumped a shipment of tea into the water. The sensational affair became known as the Boston Tea Party. King George III was alarmed over the behavior of the New Englanders, and Parliament passed a series of disciplinary measures, known by the colonists as the Intolerable Acts, in response. One of the measures called for Boston Harbor to be closed until the colonists had paid for the destroyed tea. Another measure limited the powers of the Massachusetts colonial government. British general Thomas Gage became the military governor of Massachusetts. Parliament had ordered Gage to ensure that the Intolerable Acts were enforced.

In response to this show of British force, New Englanders gathered their firearms and stored them at Lexington, Massachusetts. Such activity was unlawful, and General Gage ordered a company of

British soldiers to march to Lexington to seize the weapons. To defend themselves, New England farmers and shopkeepers organized a militia, or a citizen army. Armed with muskets, the Americans gathered to resist the British regulars, as soldiers in the British army were called. At Lexington, on April 19, 1775, the two forces exchanged gunfire that resulted in casualties on each side. The British officer in command ordered his unit to move toward Concord, Massachusetts. Along the way, American patriots fired on the marching British soldiers. At Concord, another skirmish took place before the British troops retreated to Boston.

After the December 1773 Boston Tea Party, T. M. Harris of Dorchester Neck, Massachusetts, took these tea leaves from the scene and preserved them in a glass bottle as a souvenir.

This early-twentieth-century reproduction was based on a 1784 work done by the engraver D. Berger and the artist D. Chodowiecki. The painting shows spectators cheering and observing as the rebels dump cargoes of tea into Boston Harbor on December 16, 1773.

American patriots were officially at war with Britain. The Second Continental Congress, the American governing body, met in Philadelphia, Pennsylvania, where it appointed George Washington commander in chief of the American forces on June 15, 1775.

Washington quickly rode to Boston to lead the militia that had collected there and then surrounded the British forces in a siege. British general Sir William Howe attacked the patriots at Bunker Hill on June 17, but was rebuffed. Although the British eventually won the battle and gained control of Bunker Hill, British casualties were extremely high. The continuing siege eventually forced Howe, who had replaced Gage as commander of the British forces in North America, to abandon Boston and sail his troops to Halifax, Nova Scotia, in March 1776. After the siege ended, the American militia departed from Boston and returned to their homes. General Washington was left with few men.

Congress was aware of the need to retain soldiers and create an organized fighting force. They had established the Continental army in the summer of 1775. This army was composed of men who enlisted for a year or longer. The Continental forces were the core of the American army. The state militias, upon request from the Continental Congress, would furnish militia units for short periods of service when extra men were needed.

In June 1776, General Howe returned from the north and advanced his forces on New York. After defeating

General Howe's evacuation of Boston in March 1776 was depicted by J. Godfrey and M. A. Wageman II in 1861. After Howe's departure, General Washington fortified Fort Hill, which overlooked the harbor, in case the British returned. In a March 24 letter to Congress, Washington wrote that he had made it "exceedingly difficult" for the British to land.

Washington at the Battle of Long Island on August 27, 1776, Howe took possession of New York. During the remainder of 1776, the British occupied New Jersey as well, and Americans' faith in the rebellion fell. Washington decided he must take bold action, especially as the enlistment of many of his soldiers would end on December 31.

The night of December 25, 1776, Washington carried out a surprise attack on the Hessians at Trenton, New Jersey. Hessians were professional soldiers from an area in Germany called Hesse. They had been hired by the

British to fight the Americans. Washington took his army from Pennsylvania across the icy Delaware River on December 25. On the morning after Christmas, he surprised the Hessians and inflicted a smashing defeat. A few days later on January 3, 1777, at Princeton, New Jersey, Washington gained another victory over the British. American patriots rejoiced in Washington's twin victories.

The British and American armies then set up camp for the rest of the winter. General Howe remained in New York until July 1777. The British general laid plans to capture Philadelphia, Pennsylvania. Philadelphia was a wise target because it was the unofficial capital of the

In the 1770s, Francis Xavier Habermann depicted the British occupation of New York in September 1776. A few days after the British captured the city, a fierce fire whipped though lower Manhattan and destroyed about 493 homes. Although no one was officially charged with arson, the British suspected the patriots of setting the fire.

Washington Crossing the Delaware was painted by George Caleb Bingham around 1856. The Christmas Day passage over the Delaware River was extremely uncomfortable. The Continental fleet, which set sail at dusk, encountered a winter storm with heavy winds, sleet, snow, and hail.

thirteen colonies. Philadelphia was also the seat of the Continental Congress and the largest city in America at the time. To capture Philadelphia, Howe would fight the Battle of Brandywine. It was just before this battle that Casimir Pulaski arrived in America and reported to General George Washington.

3. The Count Comes to America

Casimir Pulaski sailed from Nantes, France, on June 7, 1777, and landed in Marblehead, Massachusetts, on July 23, forty-six days later. The long voyage gave Pulaski plenty of time to consider how he might help the American cause.

After going ashore at Marblehead, the thirty-two-year-old Pulaski left for Boston and called on American commander Major General William Heath. As it is unlikely that Commissioner Benjamin Franklin knew which American general commanded in Boston, Pulaski probably asked American officers in Boston upon whom he should call.

Pulaski dined with Heath at his headquarters and quickly became aware of the disadvantages of not knowing the English language. Pulaski spoke fluent French, a language he had learned as the child of a nobleman. He managed to obtain information about the American military situation from officers present who spoke French. During his stay in Boston, Pulaski examined military fortifications that had been erected to protect the American soldiers and observed the appearance and behavior of the American soldiers.

In a letter from Boston dated July 27, 1777, Pulaski described his impressions to his friend, the French historian Claude de Rulhière: "Their artillery is in good order, but the soldiers are not well trained as they should be and the native officers lack experience." He added that the tactics of the American army were not very advanced. The recent defeats that the Americans had suffered, especially the loss of Fort Ticonderoga in New York, bothered him. British general John Burgoyne had come down from Canada to invade the fort. In the face of Burgoyne's advancing British army, American general Arthur St. Clair had abandoned the fort on July 6, 1777. Pulaski informed Rulhière that an American commander had "deserted the position" at Fort Ticonderoga and had "abandoned all his equipment and retreated without giving the slightest opposition."

Pulaski left Boston on August 3, 1777, to report to General George Washington at his headquarters at the Moland House, north of Philadelphia. He carried Benjamin Franklin's favorable letter to General Washington. Dated May 29, 1777, the letter read: "Count Pulawski of Poland, an Officer famous throughout Europe for his Bravery and Conduct in Defence of Liberties of his Country against the three great invading Powers of Russia, Austria and Prussia, will have the Honor of delivering this into your Excellency's Hands.

The Moland House was General George Washington's Pennsylvania headquarters in August 1777. The farmhouse is a stone dwelling that was originally built around 1750 by lawyer John Moland. This modern photograph shows the back exterior of the farmhouse.

The Court here have encouraged and promoted his Voyage, from an Opinion that he may be highly useful in our Service. Mr. Deane has written so fully concerning him, that I need not enlarge; and only add my Wishes, that he may find in our Armies under your Excell[enc]y, Occasions of distinguishing himself."

In addition to this letter, Pulaski had also carried from Paris a letter to the Marquis de Lafayette from his wife, Adrienne de Noailles. The twenty-year-old French nobleman had been inspired by the American cause and had

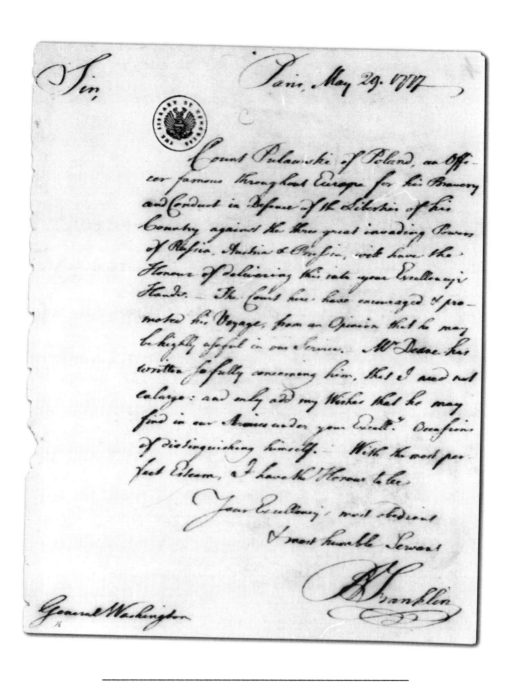

When Casimir Pulaski arrived at the Moland House in Pennsylvania, he delivered this May 29, 1777, letter of recommendation, written by Benjamin Franklin to the commander of the Continental army, General George Washington.

come to fight in the American Revolution. Pulaski delivered the letter to Lafayette, who was at Moland House meeting with General Washington. Pulaski's thoughtful deed became the occasion for a meeting with Lafayette and led to a friendship between the two men. This encounter was also fortunate as Lafayette then introduced Pulaski to General Washington.

Pulaski impressed the commander in chief. Washington drafted a letter on August 21, 1777, which Pulaski was to carry to John Hancock, the president of the Continental Congress in Philadelphia.

When Pulaski arrived in Philadelphia, he presented five letters of recommendation to the Congress. Franklin, Deane, Lafayette, Washington, and Pulaski himself had penned these five letters. Pulaski wrote in his August 24 letter to Congress, "I have passed hither from Europe to do myself the honor of being admitted among worthy Citizens in the defence of Their Country and Their Liberty." Because of his extensive experience in fighting the Russians in Poland, Pulaski asked that he initially be made commander of a volunteer cavalry company. He also asked that after he had proven himself to be a capable leader he might later be allowed to command a division.

As Pulaski waited for Congress to act on his application for service, he most likely followed the developing threat to Philadelphia. British general Sir William Howe had sailed from New York on July 23, 1777, with an army of fifteen thousand soldiers. He reappeared a month later 50 miles (20.5 km) south of Philadelphia. His objective was to capture and occupy Philadelphia, the largest American city and the heart of the rebellion. Pulaski did not wait any longer for Congress to reply. Instead he departed for the Continental army headquarters at Wilmington, Delaware.

Upon arriving, Pulaski asked that General Washington allow him to participate in the approaching battle. The commander in chief, moved by Pulaski's pleas, invited him to join his staff as a volunteer officer. Washington formally proposed that Pulaski become the first commander of cavalry of the Continental army. Washington wrote again to the president of the Continental Congress, John Hancock, on August 28: "Having endeavored at the solicitation of the Count de Pulaski, to think of some mode in employing him in our service, there is none occurs to me, liable to so few inconveniences and exceptions, as the giving him command of the horse. This department is still without a head." Washington noted that "a Man of real capacity, experience and knowledge in that service might be extremely useful." Washington highlighted Pulaski's considerable experience in cavalry operations in Poland and how this knowledge could benefit the Continental army. Before Congress acted upon Washington's recommendation, however, the Battle of the Brandywine was fought.

KOŚCIUSZKO PULAWSKI

walczyli o wolność w Ameryce. Czy ty pomożesz Ameryce walczyć o wolność w Polsce?

Jedz Mniej
Pszenicy-mięsa-tłuszczy-cukru abyśmy mogli pomodz naszym braciom walczacym w Armiach Alianckich

ZARZĄD SPOŻYWCZY STANÓW ZJEDNOCZONYCH

Thaddeus Kosciuszko, shown in a 1917 lithograph by George Illian in which Pulaski is also mentioned, was awarded U.S. citizenship. However, he returned to his homeland, Poland, in 1784.

Many Europeans came to America to help the patriots wage their war for independence. Another Pole who crossed the Atlantic Ocean was Thaddeus Kosciuszko.

After joining the Continental army, Kosciuszko contributed his engineering skill at the Battle of Saratoga in 1777 by designing a strong defensive fortification on Bemis Heights. In 1778, he supervised the two-year construction of a fort at West Point, which allowed the Americans to maintain control of the Hudson River. Toward the end of the war, Kosciuszko served as chief engineer of General Nathanael Greene's Southern army.

No evidence has yet been found that Pulaski and Kosciuszko ever met each other during their time in America. Like Pulaski, Kosciuszko was a passionate freedom fighter. In 1798, he left some $12,000 of his accumulated military pay of about $18,912 in trust for the freedom and the education of African American slaves.

The September 1777 Battle of the Brandywine was drawn by F. C. Yohn in 1898. Before the battle, Pulaski had grown impatient waiting for Congress to reply to Washington's request to make Pulaski commander of the horse. On September 3, 1777, Pulaski wrote again to Congress, "I desire to hear only yes or no . . . [what] I require of Congress is to obtain an answer to the letter from General Washington."

General Howe's army landed on the northern shore of Chesapeake Bay, Maryland. On August 28, 1777, his powerful army of approximately fifteen thousand soldiers, composed of British regulars and about five thousand Hessians, began to march north on the road toward Philadelphia. General Washington selected Chad's Ford, Pennsylvania, as the site to engage his troops, some eleven thousand men, against the enemy in battle. Chad's Ford lay about 30 miles (48.3 km) southwest of Philadelphia. Washington placed his infantry divisions along the east bank of Brandywine Creek and on both sides of Chad's Ford on September 9.

As the British army approached Chad's Ford, General Howe planned a brilliant flanking maneuver, which meant he would attack the assembled American troops from the side. Howe surrounded the Continental army on the north of their position, and he ordered the Hessians to march straight to Chad's Ford as a diversion, or an action that is taken to confuse the enemy. Meanwhile, Howe directed his subordinate General Lord Charles Cornwallis and a mass of British regulars to march north on the west bank of Brandywine Creek. As they made a wide sweep around Washington's army, the regulars were ordered to keep out of sight of the patriots.

When the Hessians reached Chad's Ford on September 11, they began a noisy artillery demonstration to give the impression that the entire British army was assembled on the west bank of Brandywine Creek. The Hessians kept up the artillery firing for several hours as Lord Cornwallis continued to encircle the Continental army without its knowledge.

When Washington finally received reports of the proximity of Lord Cornwallis, he ordered several divisions to move from their positions along Brandywine Creek and march northward to block the British advance. Nevertheless, General Howe, having gained the element of surprise and possessing a large and disciplined group of regulars, attacked the Americans and forced them to retreat. Howe planned to block the road to Chester, Pennsylvania, the Continental army's escape route.

Pulaski was anxious to help prevent what he feared might be a disastrous defeat for the Americans. Although he had no rank and no command, he pleaded with Washington to allow him to lead the thirty horsemen who formed General Washington's escort. The cavalry escort served both as the general's bodyguards and in a ceremonial role, heralding the general's stature as an important individual. Pulaski explained that he would attempt to slow down the British advance, which could potentially cut off Washington's escape as the Continental army retreated. Washington agreed.

Casimir Pulaski mounted one of the horses and directed the other horsemen to follow him. Pulaski used a technique that he had often used in Poland against the superior Russian forces. He struck the vanguard, or the soldiers in the lead, of the British advance. This unexpected attack slowed the British down as they determined the extent of the threat. Pulaski withdrew before the British realized that they were being held up by a small cavalry unit, which could easily be swept away. His actions gave the Americans the precious time they needed to retreat.

On that same day Pulaski had another opportunity to demonstrate his fighting ability and his knowledge of battle strategies. In the area of Chad's Ford, some five thousand Hessian soldiers had quickly overwhelmed the

This page from the September 1777 journals of the Continental Congress contains the appointment of Count Casimir Pulaski to commander of the horse of the Continental army on September 15.

forces of Brigadier General Anthony Wayne. The Hessians had struck after hearing the sound of firing from the north. When Pulaski discovered this problem, he hastened to Washington and asked for soldiers to strike the Hessians. Washington told Pulaski to pick up any scattered soldiers he could gather to fight. Pulaski rounded up a sizable number of men, mostly German immigrants who had settled in America, and led them in an attack. To encourage the soldiers, Pulaski shouted in German, "Vorwarts, Bruden, Vorwarts!" This rallying cry translated into English means, "Forward, brothers, forward!"

Pulaski attacked the Hessians in the flank and stopped them as they attempted to cut off General Wayne's retreat route to Chester. Pulaski's and Wayne's soldiers held the British at bay until Washington arrived and organized his retreating forces.

The day after the Battle of the Brandywine, Congress was aghast to learn of Washington's defeat. Although the battle leadership of Washington and his generals was criticized, word of Pulaski's daring exploits quickly spread among the members of Congress. Within three days of the Battle of the Brandywine, Congress awarded Count Casimir Pulaski the rank of brigadier general and an appointment as commander of the American Light Dragoons. On September 15, 1777, Congress resolved: "That a commander of the horse be appointed with the rank of brigadier; the ballots being counted, the Count Pulaski was elected."

4. Commander of the Horse

Although Casimir Pulaski was pleased with his appointment as chief commander of the American Light Dragoons, he encountered several obstacles. For one, the commander in chief of the Continental army, General George Washington, did not fully utilize the combat capability of cavalry. When four Continental cavalry regiments had been organized earlier in the war, Washington assigned these units to humble tasks, including serving as ceremonial escorts for generals or carrying messages to other divisions. Only occasionally had Washington used the cavalry appropriately as an attack force and for reconnaissance, which means scouting for the enemy on horseback and then reporting the findings back to one's commander.

One year earlier, on July 1, 1776, Major General Charles Lee had written to Washington from Charleston, South Carolina, about the potential of a mounted force, "For God's sake, my dear General, urge the Congress to furnish me with a thousand cavalry. With a thousand cavalry I could ensure the safety of these Southern

This 1899 portrait by John Faed shows General Washington acknowledging another officer's salute with his own. Historically, a sword salute had been used by the crusading knights of the Middle Ages. Before battle, a knight would respectfully kiss the top of his sword.

Provinces; and without cavalry, I can answer for nothing." Lee, second in command of the Continental army, possessed a good knowledge of cavalry operations. Lee had, in fact, served as an aide to King Poniatowski and as a major general in the Polish army from 1765 until 1769. Despite Lee's experience in the matter, Washington paid his requests little attention and he continued to underutilize the four cavalry regiments under his command.

Since the formation of the cavalry, the four colonels in charge of their respective cavalry regiments had reported directly to Washington. The busy commander in chief knew that he should assign a brigadier general to oversee them. Washington had offered the position to General Joseph Reed in January 1777, but Reed had declined. As Washington believed that none of the four cavalry colonels was deserving of the position, he left the position unfilled. The timely arrival of Casimir Pulaski seemed to have solved the problem of who should be the brigadier general of the cavalry. Luckily for Washington, Pulaski understood that the cavalry could be used as the eyes and ears of an army during reconnaissance missions and as a powerful offensive weapon during battle.

A second problem Pulaski faced as the new commander of the horse was his poor command of the English language, which hampered him from developing a rapport with his officers through casual conversation. This difficulty brought on, in part, a third difficulty, which was the animosity that many of his men and officers felt toward him. They did not like him, because he was a foreigner and because they were jealous that he had been promoted to brigadier general. In particular, three of the four

---

Following Spread: Artists often take liberties with history. This illustration from the 1800s by F. Girsch shows General Washington (*far left, wearing cloak*) with his generals at Valley Forge. Although Casimir Pulaski (*third to the right of Washington*) and Thaddeus Kosciuszko (*fourth to the right of Washington*) never met, the artist grouped them, along with other foreign officers, possibly to emphasize their great contribution.

Charles Willson Peale did this bejeweled miniature oil painting of John Laurens around 1784.

regimental commanders treated Pulaski with hostility and resentment. He was, however, able to communicate in French with Colonel Theodorick Bland, one of the regimental cavalry commanders. Their ability to communicate in a common language brought about a better understanding between the two men.

Pulaski did have allies, however. Lieutenant Colonel John Laurens, Washington's aide who spoke French and who had met Pulaski at Washington's headquarters, defended Pulaski in a March 14, 1778, letter to his father, Henry Laurens, then president of the Continental Congress: "The dislike of some of [Pulaski's] officers to him as a stranger, the advantages which they have taken of him as such, and their constant contrivances to thwart him on every occasion, made it impossible for him to command."

A fourth problem that the new commander of the horse faced was the short amount of time he had to train his men and to equip his cavalry regiments with horses. During the war, horses could often be obtained only by using impress warrants, or documents that authorized the seizure of private property for official government use.

The difficulty in obtaining horses led to a dramatic confrontation between an army officer and a prominent patriot of Maryland. In June 1778, Captain Michael Rudolph, a member of Major Henry Lee's Partisan Legion, another cavalry, demanded horses from the farm of William Paca, a signer of the Declaration of Independence. Rudolph showed Paca a document containing a vague authorization to seize his horses. Paca was furious. He later wrote the governor of Maryland: "After reading his Authority, I told him if he attempted to seize any of my horses I would blow his brains out and if he did not leave the State or cease to exercise such power I would issue my warrants and commit him to jail." Cavalry officer Rudolph left empty-handed.

Shortly after Pulaski had been appointed commander of the horse, Washington began to march his army north toward Philadelphia. On September 16, 1777, the troops stopped their march to rest. The men were exhausted and suffering from low morale after their recent defeat at Brandywine. The soldiers were given their rations and took time to eat. Pulaski, however, was concerned about the safety of the Americans' position. On his own initiative, he led a cavalry patrol in search of enemy troops. A soldier who served with Pulaski, Captain Paul Bentalou, later wrote that Pulaski "could not for a moment remain inactive . . . [and] went out with a reconnaissance party of cavalry and did not proceed very far, before he discovered the whole British army in full march upon our camp."

Alarmed, Pulaski furiously galloped back to headquarters and reported the news to Washington. General Washington had no idea that the enemy was making such a move. Some of Washington's staff made light of Pulaski's report. One of Washington's aides, Alexander Hamilton, who spoke fluent French, asked Pulaski whether he might have mistakenly identified Continental troops as British troops. Pulaski assured Hamilton that he had not. Because of Pulaski's reconnaissance, General Washington readied his army for battle. However, an unexpected storm drenched both armies with rain and prevented them from fighting. Because the ammunition was soaked and useless, the two armies marched away from each other. Thus ended what became known as the Battle of the Clouds.

Occasionally, when Pulaski rode to Washington's headquarters, he demonstrated his horsemanship for some of the staff and officers. As many of the men had ridden horses since childhood, they especially admired individuals who possessed more than usual capability. To show his skill, Pulaski would charge his horse and then hurl his gun forward as if flinging it at the enemy. Then, without losing pace, he would remove his foot from the stirrup and lean over to the ground to retrieve his pistol without the slightest effort. In Poland, Pulaski had acquired his skill and experience when he served as military commander of the Confederation of Bar. He had led his dragoons over rough terrain and often approached the unsuspecting Russian troops over ground that the enemy believed too difficult for horses to cross.

Some American historians have called Pulaski a show-off. However, Pulaski had a deeper purpose for his showmanship. He was constantly stressing to Washington, his generals, and Congress the great value of using the cavalry as a combat arm. Pulaski was demonstrating what an experienced cavalryman could do and thereby was promoting his goal.

The modern-day artist Don Troiani depicted the uniform worn by a soldier who served with the 3rd Continental Light Dragoons in 1780. The plume that extends from the soldier's helmet was made of horsehair and shielded the back of the dragoon's neck from sword blows.

5. Preparing the Cavalry for Battle

As the winter of 1777 approached, the British army settled down in Philadelphia, and Washington moved his troops to Valley Forge, Pennsylvania. The Americans suffered greatly during the winter of 1777–1778. The soldiers endured horrible cold and starvation from lack of supplies. During this winter lull in fighting, Pulaski began to organize a program of exercise and discipline for his men. He was aided in this training by two of his officers: Francois-Louis Teissedre de Fleury, a Frenchman, and Jan Zielinski, an experienced cavalryman who had fought in Pulaski's army of the Confederation of Bar in Poland.

Not only were the soldiers hungry during the winter of 1777–1778, but also the horses were starving. In Poland, Pulaski had taken excellent care of his horses. The condition of the horses in America saddened him. General Washington agreed with Pulaski about the unhappy state of the cavalry at Valley Forge. He ordered Pulaski on December 31, 1777, to march his four cavalry regiments to Trenton, New Jersey, where

Valley Forge, Pennsylvania, the headquarters of the Continental army from December 1777 through June 1778, is a modern-day national historic park. The log cabins were rebuilt according to historical sources and artifacts found at the original camp. At left, a group of men dressed as Continental army soldiers participate in a reenactment.

there might be more food for the horses. Pulaski was to seek lodging for his soldiers among the civilian population. Washington reminded the young general to continue training his cavalry.

When Pulaski arrived in Trenton on January 9, he found little available housing for his men and a scarcity of forage, or food for domestic animals such as horses. Sailors from the military had also been instructed to winter in Trenton, New Jersey, and had already taken much of the housing for themselves. Except for a small

This panel from around 1760 was painted by the English artist Thomas Butler. The drawings were based on earlier illustrations by John Vanderbank contained in a 1729 book on dressage. Dressage is a French word that means training, most frequently, the training of a horse.

Though historians do not know if Pulaski practiced dressage, many horsemen from Europe were trained in the art. The precise control a rider gained over his horse through dressage was invaluable in battle.

The Manege Gallop with the Right Leg (*top*) refers to maneuvering one's horse around a manege. A manege is a place where horses are instructed in the precise movements of dressage.

Terre a Terre to the Right (*bottom*) depicts a rider directing his horse in a slow, high-stepping movement, forward and to the right.

detachment of cavalry, which remained in Trenton, Pulaski stationed the four regiments outside of the town. Pulaski, as leader of the cavalry, would remain in Trenton.

Because the inexperience of the troops worried Pulaski, he drilled his men in the rudiments of horsemanship. Pulaski selected the horseman Colonel Michael Kovatch for the position of master of exercise of the dragoons. Michael Kovatch was a Hungarian who had served in the Royal Prussian Army, where he had gained the rank of captain of hussars. Most of the men Pulaski chose to help him were men he knew personally and who were also veterans of European wars. A number of these men had fought with him against the Russians.

The lance had been a favorite weapon of the Polish cavalry. As part of his plan to improve the American cavalry, Pulaski proposed to Washington the organization of a special squadron of lancemen, or horsemen who were equipped with lances similar to those carried by medieval knights. Pulaski himself would command this squadron.

Casimir Pulaski began to train a squadron of 120 lancers with the help of his master of exercise, Kovatch. The lancers had been selected from each of the four cavalry regiments. Although the lance, or spear, was routinely used in Europe, Americans found it strange. The lance had a long wooden shaft with a pointed iron head. Some inexperienced American

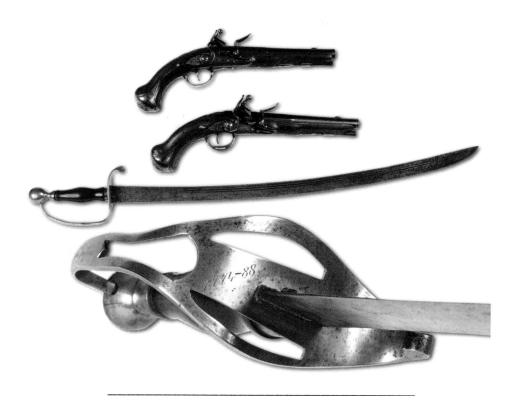

The pistol and the saber were frequently used by the cavalry in the American Revolution. The officers' pistols were made sometime in the 1700s. The iron and brass saber was made around 1770. The hilt of this saber, shown in closeup, was inscribed with the name and years of service of the owner, Lt. Col. John Griffin, 1774–1788.

lancers lost their balance carrying the lance and fell from their horses. Americans preferred the sword, which was smaller and easier to maneuver than the lance.

While Kovatch tutored the lancemen, Pulaski conducted his own rigorous training. He had the Prussian cavalry drill manuals translated into English and used these exercises to prepare his ragged, untrained brigade for the spring military campaigns. Meanwhile, Pulaski also continued his ongoing efforts to persuade Washington that the Continental army needed a cavalry

Although a mounted cavalry soldier had some advantages over foot soldiers, such as advancing on the enemy with speed and employing a saber from the height of a horse, a cavalry soldier had to control his animal in the heat of battle. Both the soldier and his mount were trained to work together in combat. In training, a horse was exposed to the explosive sound of a fired pistol until the animal eventually learned not to fear gunfire.

The metal sabers used by the cavalry were heavy. A soldier had to practice swinging a saber without losing his balance and falling from his horse. As the enemy might either be mounted or running toward him on the ground, a soldier learned how to use his weapon from different heights. Some soldiers practiced this skill by slashing at wooden logs that had been driven into the ground.

When the cavalry charged the enemy as a unit, the horse and rider had to remain in formation. The commander might order his unit to move to the left, to the right, to wheel about, or to come to a halt. The cavalrymen were drilled in these formations before they used them in battle.

force superior in number and capability to that of the British if the Americans were to win the war.

Some of Pulaski's cavalrymen resented the preparatory training and drills to which they were subjected. A few of the officers took their complaints to the commander in chief. Washington wrote to Pulaski on January 26, 1778: "Your Officers complain that the Cavalry undergo severer duty now, than they did while they were in Camp. As rest and refreshment are two of the principal objects of your removal from camp, I hope you will by proper arrangement give your Men and Horses an opportunity of reaping these benefits from their Winter Quarters."

In a February 24 letter to his sister Anna in Poland, Casimir revealed his frustration and the resentment he had experienced since his arrival in America seven months before: "The people here are too jealous; in the whole army everyone is against me." On that same day Pulaski wrote another letter to his friend Claude de Rulhière in France: "Here I command the cavalry, but I am not very happy. I rack my brain to accomplish my duty and equip them, but it is hopeless." Pulaski also described the hostility of many American officers: "Foreigners are not liked here and they are tolerated only so long as it is necessary." His most telling statement in this letter centered on his decision to resign as commander: "I have decided to quit this army."

Four days later, on February 28, Count Casimir Pulaski drafted a letter of resignation to General

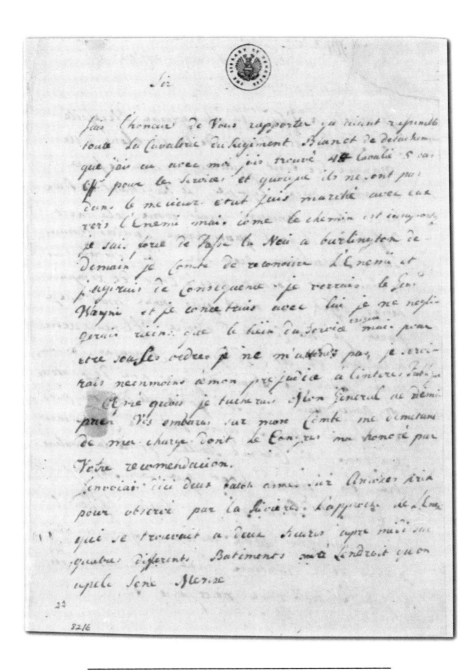

This February 28, 1778, letter from Count Casimir Pulaski to George Washington was written in French. Although Pulaski gave his resignation, he was still concerned about equipping his soldiers: "I repeat to Your Excellency the very great necessity of attending to the needs of the cavalry. They lack everything."

Washington. Pulaski suggested that Colonel Theodorick Bland might replace him as commander of the horse.

Before Pulaski had written his letter of resignation, however, he had been ordered by General Washington to aid Brigadier General Anthony Wayne at Haddonfield, New Jersey. Wayne had learned that a British force of some two thousand regulars was advancing on him. Earlier, Washington had ordered Wayne to search for food, supplies, horses, and forage around Philadelphia. Wayne was instructed to protect these critical supplies and to ensure that they made their way to the starving Continental army at Valley Forge.

The success of Wayne's mission in the winter of 1777–1778 was crucial to the survival of Washington's army. In striking contrast to Washington's earlier note instructing Pulaski to rest his troops, Washington ordered Pulaski into action. Although few of Pulaski's soldiers were fit for combat, Pulaski managed to assemble a capable group of forty-four dragoons and five officers for the mission.

Casimir Pulaski and his small unit joined General Wayne at Mount Holly, New Jersey, and together they marched to Haddonfield where they found a strong British outpost located at a mill.

Pulaski was eager to attack the enemy. Wayne hesitated, however, as he considered the odds too great. Not waiting for Wayne to make up his mind whether to attack, Pulaski and his small force charged the British

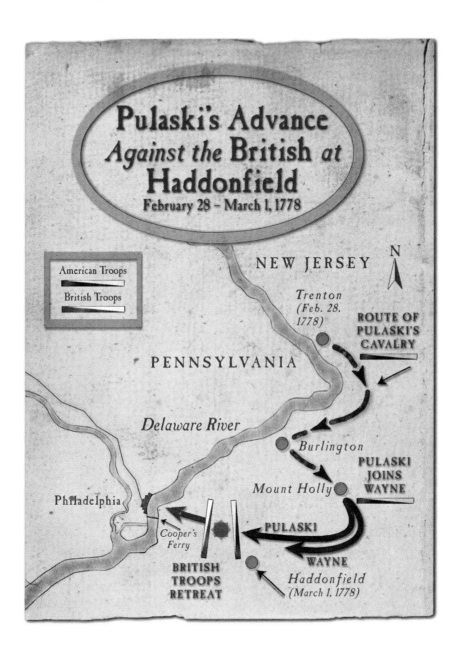

This map shows the progression of Pulaski and Wayne's combined forces as they advanced on the British troops in Haddonfield, New Jersey. The outnumbered Continental force still managed to drive the British into a retreat toward Philadelphia. This victory allowed them to gather much-needed supplies for Washington's army.

troops in a surprise night attack on March 1, 1778. The British were alarmed by what they believed might be a superior force of Continental troops and quickly retreated. Pulaski wanted to chase after the retreating enemy, but Wayne restrained him. Pulaski's actions had compelled the British commander Colonel Stirling to withdraw to Philadelphia.

Pulaski had not only saved Wayne from probable defeat but had also helped the starving army at Valley Forge. The *New Jersey Gazette*, on March 11, 1778, gleefully described the British retreat: "happiest was the Briton who had the longest legs and the nimblest heads. Leaving bag and baggage, they retreated precipitately to Cooper's Ferry." Anthony Wayne praised Pulaski's performance in a March 4, 1778, letter to Washington: "Genl. Pulaski behaved with his usual bravery on the Occasion." Pulaski informed Washington of the loss of ten horses, four killed, three totally disabled, and three slightly wounded. Pulaski lost his own horse, a costly and magnificent steed that was shot in the leg and disabled. His dragoons, however, had escaped unharmed.

On March 3, 1778, Washington acknowledged Pulaski's resignation as commander of the horse. Washington wrote: "Your intention to resign is founded on reasons which I presume make you think the measure necessary. I can only say therefore that it will always give me pleasure to bear testimony of the zeal and Bravery which you displayed on every occasion."

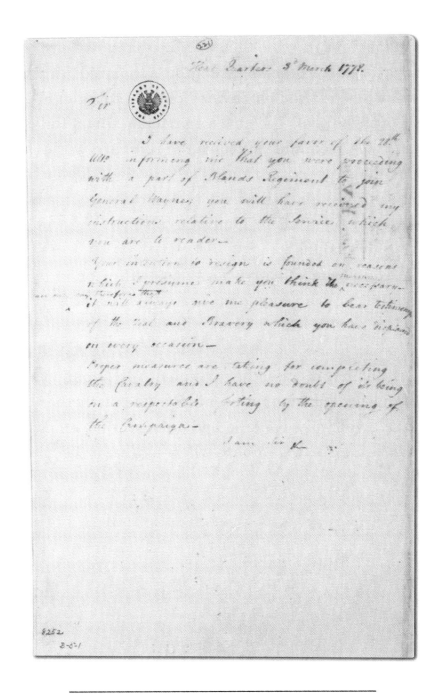

In his March 3, 1778, letter to Casimir Pulaski, General Washington assured Pulaski that, if Pulaski resigned as commander of the horse, Washington would see to it that the cavalry were properly equipped and "on a respectable footing by the opening of the campaign."

Pulaski returned to the main army that was assembled at Valley Forge. Washington appointed Stephen Moylan, one of the four cavalry regimental colonels, to take over the post. The new commander, whom Pulaski greatly disliked, did not continue the hard work that Pulaski had put into training the cavalry. Moylan had poor leadership skills and lacked the professional dedication required to ready his men for the coming spring campaigns.

Washington quickly became disillusioned with Moylan's lack of leadership and criticized him in an April 11, 1778, letter: "Your return of the Cavalry is really vexatious." Dissatisfied with Moylan and having a low opinion of the other regimental commanders of the brigade, Washington eventually had no further use for the cavalry. By 1779, he had ordered what remained of the regiments to the South where forage for the horses was more available.

6. The Pulaski Legion

Although Casimir Pulaski resigned as commander of the Continental cavalry, he did not abandon the cause of American independence. Pulaski decided to create an independent legion that reported directly to Washington or another army commander. The cavalry brigade he had previously commanded consisted of four separate regiments, each under a separate commanding officer. As Pulaski had complained to his friend Rulhière, "Our cavalry is forever dispersed in small groups and when we must fight, we are reduced to nothing."

At Valley Forge, Pulaski spoke with Washington about organizing a separate group of horsemen. Washington supported Pulaski's continued service and wrote to the president of the Continental Congress, Henry Laurens, on March 14, 1778, that Pulaski's character and service entitled him to retain the rank of brigadier general in a newly formed unit. Washington also stated, "I have only to add that the Count's valour and active zeal on all occasions have

A double-sided crimson silk banner was embroidered with gold silk thread by the Moravian sisters in 1778. At the center of this banner (*shown is a recreation of the original*) were the initials "U.S.," which stand for the United States.

When Casimir Pulaski visited his recruiting station in Bethlehem, Pennsylvania, in April 1778, he and his second in command, Colonel Kovatch, entered a chapel during evening services. The chapel was part of a Moravian settlement, a religious group of men and women who had immigrated to America from Bohemia and Germany.

Pulaski spoke briefly with the Moravian sisters, or nuns, after the service. Later, Pulaski instructed his men to protect the Moravian sisters' house from the rough soldiers who were stationed in the area.

In appreciation, the sisters made an embroidered silken banner for the legion to carry into battle. On one side of the banner the sisters had embroidered Unita Virtus Fortior, Latin for "United, Valor Is Stronger." On the opposite side, alongside the seeing eye of God, were the words Non Alius Regit, which means "No Other Governs."

GENERAL CASIMIR PULASKI AND OFFICERS OF HIS LEGION AT BETHLEHEM IN THE SPRING OF 1778 RECEIVE THE BANNER MADE FOR THEM HERE BY THE MORAVIAN SINGLE SISTERS

In 1937, George Gray depicted the Moravian Sisters presenting the banner to Casimir Pulaski and his officers. Moravian missionaries established a settlement in Bethlehem, Pennsylvania, in 1741. Many of the Moravian missionaries came to North America hoping to convert the Native Americans to Christianity.

done him great honor; and . . . he will render great Services with such a Command as he asks for; I wish him to succeed in his application." Lieutenant Colonel John Laurens, an aide to Washington, also supported Pulaski's proposal and urged his father, Henry Laurens, to approve it. After explaining the purpose and composition of the legion, Laurens ended his note with praise for the Pole: "His zeal for our cause and courage, proof against every danger will cover him with glory, and I hope promote the general interest."

Pulaski traveled to York, Pennsylvania, where

Francois Godefroy did this engraving of a meeting of the First Continental Congress, which was held at Carpenters' Hall in Philadelphia. The artist based his work on an earlier eighteenth-century engraving done by the artist Le Barbier.

Congress had relocated after the British had occupied Philadelphia, and presented his plan for an independent legion of cavalry. The Continental Congress president, Henry Laurens, referred the plan to the Board of War president, General Horatio Gates. General Gates approved the plan and then passed it on for comment to Major General Charles Lee, who enthusiastically endorsed it. On March 28, 1778, Congress resolved that Count Pulaski "have command of an independent corps," consisting of sixty-eight cavalry soldiers and two hundred infantrymen.

Pulaski set up three different recruiting stations, in Baltimore, Maryland; Trenton, New Jersey; and Easton, Pennsylvania. Washington also allowed Pulaski to choose two men from each of the four existing cavalry regiments and to select his own officers. Pulaski was eager to complete the enlistment, train his men, and then enter the soldiers in battle. Although the legion had a few American officers, the majority were European. Many of these men had previously been unwelcome in the Continental army.

Equipping the cavalry and infantry was perhaps the more challenging task. As a combat unit, the legion required horses, weapons, uniforms, and camp equipment. Congress began to provide money for Pulaski. Whenever Congress failed to offer funds promptly, Pulaski used his own money, money that his family sent him from Poland, to help pay his legion's considerable expenses. Horses were especially costly.

On one occasion, Captain Paul Bentalou, a member of the legion, had to pay $400 for a horse. Even General Washington complained about the price of horses, including nags, or horses that were considered old and sickly. Washington remarked, "A Rat in the shape of a horse is not to be bought at this time for less than £200." To safeguard his costly investment in horses, Pulaski had them branded with the initials "I.L." for Independent Legion.

On July 29, 1778, Pulaski presented the new legion for the first time to the Maryland state officials and the civilians of Baltimore. A newspaper reported that the legion "performed many Manoeuvres in a manner that reflected the highest Honour on both officers and privates." The soldiers wore dark blue coats, sleeve waistcoats, and cloaks of blue and gray. They wore helmets and black turbans decorated with a star, white feathers, and horsehair crests, and leather breeches with polished black boots. The infantry wore gaiters, or leg coverings, and white smallcoats. On every soldier's uniform sewn across the front and on the sleeves were white buttons marked "USA" and silver buttons stamped "PL" for "Pulaski Legion." The light infantry, soldiers who were lightly equipped for rapid marching, carried muskets, bayonets, and tomahawks. The cavalry was armed with sabers, pistols, rifled carbines, and lances.

By the end of July, Pulaski had still not received final acceptance of his assembled legion by Congress.

This Philadelphia street scene, *Back of the State House,* was engraved by William Birch around 1798. Another name for the State House was Independence Hall. Delegates to Congress drafted both the Declaration of Independence and the U.S. Constitution at Independence Hall.

Therefore on August 25, 1778, Pulaski proudly marched about 268 men into Philadelphia. Congress had returned to the capital after General Howe and his forces had left Philadelphia that same spring to advance toward New York. The delegates of Congress gathered outside the doors of Independence Hall and watched the military procession, which attracted a crowd of spectators who cheered the splendid-looking legionnaires. The delegates of Congress were impressed. General Pulaski and his Independent Legion were ready to join Washington's army.

7. Betrayal at Little Egg Harbor

On October 5, 1778, Congress directed Pulaski to defend the region around Little Egg Harbor, an inlet along the east coast of New Jersey. American privateers had established a base there, and periodically the privateers would sail from the harbor to raid British ships in the Atlantic Ocean. Privateers were armed ships, owned by private citizens, that often served their country in times of war by stealing cargo and supplies that were destined for the enemy. So successful were the privateers that the British called their base a "nest of rebel pirates." British general Sir Henry Clinton had been directed by the British government to destroy the privateers. Clinton ordered a squadron of ships to sail to Little Egg Harbor. The British ships sailed from New York on September 30, 1778. Congress learned of the enemy's advance a few days later and on October 5 dispatched orders to Pulaski at Trenton. Congress also called in Colonel Thomas Proctor's artillery regiment in Philadelphia and the New Jersey militia to assist Pulaski. Upon receiving his orders, Pulaski marched his legion to Little Egg Harbor.

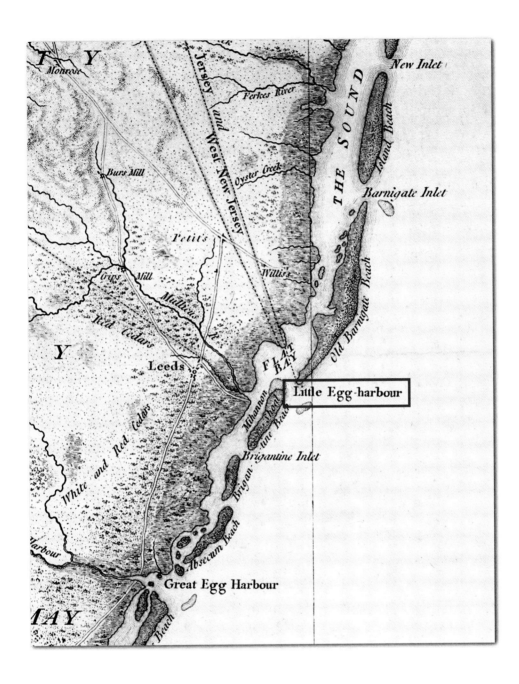

This closeup of a 1778 map of New Jersey was engraved by William Faden in London. The mapmaker based his work on several surveys of the region, including a military survey done by British and Hessian troops stationed in the area. A blue box highlights Little Egg Harbor.

On the evening of October 5, the British ships arrived at Little Egg Harbor. For the next two days, the landing force of four hundred British soldiers destroyed many of the privateers' storehouses and ships. Captain Patrick Ferguson, commanding the raid, also planned to attack important American ironworks at Batsto, about 15 miles (24 km) inland from the harbor. Ferguson abandoned the attempt when British loyalists in the area warned him of the rapid advance of Pulaski's Legion. The British troops returned to their ships on the evening of October 7, but high winds prevented them from sailing away. Pulaski reached Little Egg Harbor the next day.

Pulaski set up camp within sight of the British ships that were anchored in the bay. Trees camouflaged his troops so that the British could not see the Americans from the sea. A little more than one-quarter of a mile (0.4 km) from Pulaski's main camp, Lieutenant Colonel Carl Von Bose, the legion's infantry commander, and fifty Continental soldiers occupied a picket post.

E. Sack created this late-1800s watercolor of a Hessian soldier by copying an earlier 1778 work done by Captain Friedrich von Germann.

From there they defended the American camp. Conditions remained quiet until an explosive argument between Lieutenant Colonel Carl Von Bose and Lieutenant Carl Wilhelm Juliat led to tragic consequences. Juliat, a Hessian, had defected to the American side and was assigned by Congress to Pulaski's Legion. Von Bose criticized Juliat for deserting the Hessian army.

Juliat was furious and plotted his revenge. Shortly after the confrontation with Von Bose, Juliat pretended to go fishing. He took along four other soldiers, two of whom knew of Juliat's plans. The other two men believed they were really going fishing. The group rowed out to the British ships in the harbor and boarded the *Nautilus*. Juliat disclosed to the squadron commander Henry Colins and Captain Ferguson the strength and exact locations of Pulaski's infantry and cavalry. Juliat proposed to lead an attack on the American picket post. The two British officers agreed.

On the night of October 14, 1778, Ferguson, Juliat, and 250 British soldiers boarded small boats and rowed to shore, arriving on land about 3:00 A.M. Quietly they advanced to the picket post, where Juliat's primary goal was to assault Von Bose. The British attacked the sleeping legionnaires with bayonets. Captain Paul Bentalou of Pulaski's Legion later wrote: "On the first alarm the Lieut. Colonel [Von Bose] rushed out, armed with his sword and pistols, but though he was a remarkably stout man, and fought like a lion, he was over powered by numbers and killed." When the sounds of attack reached Pulaski's headquarters, he rounded up the cavalry and galloped to the picket post. Ferguson did not tarry, however. After accomplishing his mission, he broke off the fighting and retreated with his men into the darkness.

General Pulaski reported the British attack to Congress. Sadly he reported the loss of about thirty legionnaires killed, wounded, or missing, as well as the deaths of Lieutenant Colonel Von Bose and Lieutenant Joseph de la Borderie. Pulaski identified Juliat as the betrayer and reported taking several prisoners. Pulaski buried the two officers and the slain soldiers in a common grave at the scene of the slaughter.

From November 1778 to January 1779, Pulaski's Legion was stationed at Minisink, New York, a heavily forested frontier on the Delaware River between New York and Pennsylvania. The settlers in the region feared attacks by the aggressive Seneca Indians, and Washington ordered Pulaski to provide military protection. Pulaski carried out Washington's orders even though cavalry could not be used effectively against Native Americans hiding in the bush. Pulaski believed his powerful cavalry was being wasted in the wilderness. In his mind, the real enemy was the British army, not the Native Americans. In January, Washington needed to find a place for Pulaski's horsemen to camp for the winter. Washington finally directed Pulaski to march his cavalry to Wilmington, Delaware, and await further orders. Most

A GENERAL RETURN of the Strength in Men and Horses of the United States of America, commanded by

(Philadelphia: Printed by JOHN DUNLAP, of whom may be had all Kinds of BLANKS for the ARMY)

Regiment of Light Horse, in the Service of the the Day of 1779

Field Officers.
- Colonel.
- Lieutenant Colonel.
- Major.
- Chaplain.

Staff Officers.
- Surgeon.
- Surgeon's Mate.
- Pay Master.
- Adjutant.
- Quarter-Master.

Commiss. Off.
- Captain.
- Lieutenant.
- Cornet.

Non-Commissi. Officers.
- Quarter Master Serjeant.
- Serjeant.
- Corporals.
- Trumpet Major.
- Trumpeters.
- Sadler.
- Farrier.

Rank and File.
- Present fit for Duty.
- Sick Present.
- Sick Absent.
- Sick in Hospital.
- On Command.
- On Furlough.
- Confined.
- Dead.
- Deserted.
- Discharged.
- Total.

Wanting to Compleat.
- Serjeant.
- Corporal.
- Trumpet Major.
- Trumpeter.
- Farrier.
- Sadler.
- Rank and File.
- Supernumerary

Horses.
- Present fit for Duty.
- Sick Present.
- Sick Absent.
- Lame.
- Dead.
- Strayed.
- Unfit for Service.
- Total.
- Wanting to complete.

ABSENTEES.

Officers Names.	Rank.	By what means Absent.	Time of Absence.	Recruiting Parties.

John Dunlap of Philadelphia, Pennsylvania, printed this accounting of the men and the horses in Count Casimir Pulaski's regiment of light horse cavalry as of October 10, 1779.

of Pulaski's men left immediately. Pulaski's infantry, however, briefly remained on duty at Minisink.

The legion remained split for only a short time, because Britain soon launched a major campaign in the South. The British planned to conquer the southern colonies and then advance on the North. King George III counted on the sizable loyalist population in the South to support his campaign. On February 2, 1779, Congress ordered Pulaski to march his legion to South Carolina, where he would serve under General Benjamin Lincoln, the commander of the Southern Department of the Continental army.

Pulaski looked forward to the assignment. He would, however, have to march his troops a distance of 700 miles (1,126.5 km), the first long journey for any American unit in the war. Pulaski wrote Congress and made several requests. He asked that arrangements be made so that his horses would have enough grass and hay to eat along the journey. Some horses would also need to be replaced, as the animals might tire or become ill during the long march. Pulaski asked that he be authorized to recruit additional men since his legion was under-manned. The Board of War agreed to his requests.

Among the new officers that Pulaski recruited was Alexander O'Neil, an Irish-French man. O'Neil had served as a major under Pulaski in Poland and had an extensive military background. Pulaski also selected Captain Lewis Celeron, a Canadian who had served in the Continental army for two years. Celeron admired Pulaski and asked to serve in General Pulaski's corps, even as a volunteer. Baron George Gustave d'Ugglaa, another foreign volunteer and a Swedish nobleman, specifically asked the Board of War to assign him to Pulaski's Legion.

During the march to the South, Pulaski's troops behaved properly with respect to the civilians. Pulaski's instructions to his command and the presence of his experienced officers ensured discipline in the legionnaires. Many southerners were seeing military uniforms for the first time. The legionnaires found the people friendly and were often greeted with food and smiles.

At the beginning of May 1779, the Legion entered South Carolina. As Pulaski neared Charleston, he began to receive reports of British general Augustin Prevost's movements. After sparring with American general Benjamin Lincoln's army in Georgia, Prevost had marched his British army north into South Carolina with the intention of capturing the city of Charleston. As Lincoln was still some distance away, near Augusta, Georgia, Casimir Pulaski took it upon himself to defend Charleston.

In the 1700s, Mather Brown painted General Augustin Prevost wearing his British uniform.

8. The Cavalry Saves Charleston, South Carolina

In early May 1779, when British general Augustin Prevost marched his army into South Carolina and moved toward Charleston, the state and city officials debated whether to fight the British or surrender. Governor John Rutledge of South Carolina estimated the city's available military force. There were four hundred militia under the command of General William Moultrie and about one thousand more troops that Rutledge had recently recruited to defend the city.

During this time, Casimir Pulaski ordered his infantry to march to Charleston. Pulaski and the cavalry, riding ahead of the infantry, arrived at Charleston on May 8, 1779. The infantry reached the city three days later.

On May 11, British troops arrived 12 miles (19.3 km) north of Charleston and then continued to the outskirts of the city. The governor was alarmed over the potential devastation the British might inflict on the townspeople and their property, as well as the damage they might wreak on the plantations in the state. The state's Privy Council voted five to three to surrender the city without a fight. Rutledge sent a message to Prevost stating the terms of surrender. The terms he proposed were favorable for the British but disastrous for the Americans.

The two army generals, Pulaski and Moultrie, protested vigorously to the governor when they learned the terms of the surrender. What Rutledge and the Privy Council offered the British was the neutrality of South Carolina during the war. These terms, if accepted, would take South Carolina out of the war effort and deny the patriots

Robert Hinckley painted Governor John Rutledge around 1888. Hinckley based his painting on an earlier work done by John Trumbull around 1791.

the use of a major seaport in the South. Pulaski told Rutledge, "As a Continental officer, I will defend the city for the United States."

Pulaski had a bold plan. He would attack Prevost briefly so that the British general might pause to assess the situation. If Pulaski managed to stall the British regulars for a day or two, his willingness to defend the city might reinforce the resistance of those South Carolinians who still wanted to fight for independence. Pulaski laid plans for a trap. He would place eighty infantry in a valley behind an embankment that was screened with

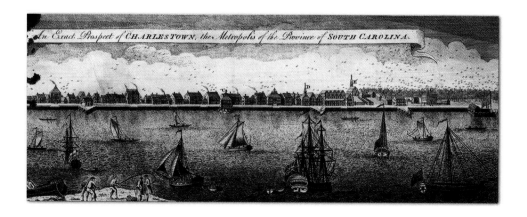

This panorama, or extended view, of the waterfront of Charleston, South Carolina, appeared in a London magazine in 1762. The illustration may have served as a guide to Europeans interested in visiting or learning about the city, as the artist labeled Charleston's prominent buildings with letters.

shrubs and then ride forward with his dragoons to meet the British advance. Then, pretending to retreat, he would bait the enemy to pursue his cavalry just past the ambush. A tremendous volley of fire would then cut the British down.

On May 11, 1779, after placing the infantry in position under the command of Lieutenant Colonel Charles Bedaulx, Casimir Pulaski rode forward with the cavalry to locate the British. About 1 mile (1.6 km) north of Charleston, the cavalry attacked a large force of British dragoons. Both sides engaged in a fierce battle, one of the few cavalry fights in the American Revolution. The battlefield was chaotic. Sabers slashed, lances pierced the enemy, and sounds of pistols cracked. Meanwhile, Bedaulx, who lay in wait for the planned ambush, heard the sounds of the fight. Eager to fight, or perhaps too anxious to remain still, Bedaulx abandoned the planned ambush and rushed to join the battle. Pulaski's plan for an ambush was destroyed. Soon Bedaulx's infantry was engulfed by swarms of British regulars. The engagement was lost, and Pulaski ordered the survivors to retreat.

Pulaski never relayed Bedaulx's misjudgment to Governor Rutledge, General Moultrie, or Congress. As Legion commander, Pulaski took the blame upon himself. He had selected his officers, they were his companions, and he took responsibility for their actions. Most of the eighty infantrymen were killed, wounded, or captured. Colonel Michael Kovatch, second in command, was severely wounded in the fight and died immediately afterward. Captain Jan Zielinski was seriously wounded while charging the British with his company of lancers. He died from his wounds five months later in a Charleston hospital.

Although Pulaski's bold attack against the British cost his legion dearly, his actions gained the Americans valuable time. While Prevost was deciding whether to advance and capture Charleston, he received reports of the approach of General Lincoln's army. If Prevost remained at Charleston, he would soon be battling both the defenders of the city and Lincoln's advancing Continental army. During the night of May 11–12, 1779, the British general quietly withdrew his soldiers from Charleston.

9. The Siege of Savannah

After British general Prevost withdrew his army, he made his way to the James and Johns Islands, located near Charleston. Casimir Pulaski and his cavalry followed Prevost and reported the British movement to General Moultrie, who then passed the information to General Lincoln. As Lincoln's army approached the British forces, Prevost assembled his soldiers and started building redoubts, or temporary defensive fortifications, at Stono River Ferry, also in South Carolina. Pulaski surveyed the British position and calculated that the British forces were too strong for an American strike.

A few days passed while Pulaski awaited Lincoln's decision. Lincoln consulted with Governor Rutledge, increased his forces, and then attacked the British defensive position at Stono River Ferry on James Island on June 20, 1779.

The attack, which resulted in heavy American casualties, caused Prevost to hasten his troops on to Savannah, Georgia, which had fallen into British hands the previous year. In July, Pulaski returned to Charleston to recuperate from an illness. He and other members of the legion may have contracted an illness after their exposure to the marshy and mosquito-infested waters of South Carolina. Both the American and British armies ceased fighting and rested to escape the summer's steamy heat. During the war, volunteer soldiers were only required to serve for three months at a time. During the break, many of the volunteers took the opportunity to leave. When the American militia went home, the southern army dwindled to a small force. Only Pulaski's Legion and two battalions of South Carolinian Continentals remained in the area.

Count Charles D'Estaing, painted by Jean Baptiste Lebrun in 1769, was commissioned as a French admiral in 1767.

As the end of summer approached, French admiral Count Charles D'Estaing's naval fleet was fighting British forces in the West Indies, over the possession of several islands. France had officially joined the patriot's battle against the British in June 1778. American and French officials such as Governor Rutledge, Colonel Marquis de Bretigny, a French officer of the Continental army, and Monsieur Plombard, the French consul in Charleston, urged D'Estaing to employ his powerful navy and soldiers to capture Savannah, Georgia.

The admiral agreed to this request, but said the combined French and American forces must attack soon, as the French fleet could not remain in the South Atlantic once the hurricane season began. D'Estaing sent General Viscount de Fontages to Charleston to coordinate a joint plan of attack. As Lincoln prepared to move his army to Savannah, the French fleet reached the mouth of the Savannah River on September 8, 1779. The French had 4,000 soldiers. Combined, the French and American allies would have 5,000 troops. The British had concentrated 3,200 soldiers in the region to defend Savannah.

D'Estaing initially brought ashore 1,200 troops at the Beaulieu Plantation, which was located 13 miles (20.9 km) south of Savannah. Pulaski and his cavalry met the admiral when he came ashore and then led the French forces until they were within 3 miles (4.8 km) of the city where D'Estaing set up camp. During that same day other French troops continued to come ashore.

D'Estaing, who wanted to capture Savannah on his own, sent a message to British general Prevost demanding that he surrender. Prevost cleverly stalled for time, saying first that he had to consult with the British royal governor of Georgia and then later that he required a twenty-four-hour truce before he made such an important decision. D'Estaing agreed.

Opposite: Admiral D'Estaing ordered Pierre Ozanne to create this 1779 French map in preparation for a combined French and American assault on the besieged city of Savannah. The inset is an enlarged area of the map that shows the position of Pulaski's dragoons.

Prevost's tactics gave the British more time to build fortifications around Savannah and allowed for an additional 800 British soldiers at Beaufort, South Carolina, to reach the city. When Prevost finally felt his forces were sufficient, he sent word to the admiral that he refused to surrender.

Had the French admiral attacked earlier, the combined French and American forces might have captured the city. Finally, D'Estaing and Lincoln decided to make their move. The French positioned themselves about 300 yards (274.3 m) from the British fortifications. On October 3, 1779, the allies began to bombard the city with 33 cannons and 9 mortars. The roar of the assault lasted for five days. During the Continental forces' siege of Savannah, Lincoln ordered Casimir Pulaski to attack a group of British troops situated near the Ogeechee River, about 12 miles (19.3 km) south of the city. Pulaski rode out with his cavalry and burst upon the enemy camp. He captured several British soldiers. The rest of the soldiers fled to the safety of their ships on the river.

The pounding cannons and mortars did not force the British to surrender Savannah. Anxious to sail away before he was trapped by bad weather, D'Estaing decided to assault the city and planned an attack with Lincoln. The French were to employ 3,500 troops. The Americans would devote 600 Continentals, including Pulaski's cavalry, and 250 Charleston militia. The main point of attack would be near the center of the British fortifications at an area called Spring Hill.

The plan was a good one. However, the night before the attack, a Charleston soldier named Sergeant Major James Curry deserted to the British and revealed the plan to Prevost, including the allies' main point of attack. Curry might have been a loyalist who served the British by spying on the Americans. With this information, Prevost was able to prepare in advance for the attack. He rearranged his soldiers and placed a great many more soldiers around Spring Hill.

During the early hours of October 9, 1779, French and American forces marched through swamps and rice fields to their assigned positions. A French unit flanked the British from the left, and an American unit flanked them from the right. The main attack of allied soldiers had been arranged in columns and approached the fortifications straight up the center. D'Estaing led the center forces himself.

Pulaski's cavalry occupied a position to the left of Spring Hill. His role in the battle plan was to charge into the city once D'Estaing had made him an opening. The cavalry would cause alarm and confusion behind enemy lines. Pulaski's Legion would charge through the streets cutting down foot soldiers from behind. The combined French and American troops battling outside the city would continue to press forward over the fortifications until the British defenses collapsed. D'Estaing and Lincoln's plan was excellent, and they expected to surprise the enemy at their main point of attack, Spring Hill.

When 250 French troops attacked at Spring Hill, the British, prepared for the assault, immediately repulsed them. Meanwhile, the two columns led by D'Estaing were stalled by British fire. The French unit on the left near the Savannah River could only move eighty of its soldiers forward. The rest of the men got stuck in a swamp, and were unable to effectively join the attack. The British continued to pour musketry and cannon fire into the attackers. British warships anchored in the Savannah River added to the cannon fire.

The British infantry ferociously defended their position. Each time the French and American columns reached the fortifications, the British counterattacked and pushed them back. French and American casualties were enormous. Even Admiral D'Estaing suffered wounds in the arm and leg. Without the admiral to lead them, the French soldiers began to waver.

During this time, Pulaski anxiously awaited word that he could approach through an opening in the British line of fortifications. Instead, he learned that Admiral D'Estaing had been grievously wounded. Pulaski and several of his officers decided to find D'Estaing. He planned to rally the disorganized French troops and lead them in another charge against the

British defense. As Pulaski galloped closer to Spring Hill, he entered an area of intense shelling. The cavalry commander had faced enemy bullets in Poland and America. Each time he had escaped death. On this day, Count Casimir Pulaski's luck ran out. The Pole gasped with pain and fell off his horse. He had been struck in the groin by a shell the size of a small iron ball. The shell may have been fired from one of the British warships on the Savannah River.

Amid the hail of bullets, Pulaski was carried a short distance away from the area of intense fire. Colonel

Pulaski at Savannah was painted by Stanislaw Batowski in 1933. A soldier who had fought alongside Casimir Pulaski and witnessed his actions in combat said, "The Count in battle—how he seemed to fight as if enjoying a banquet; how, again and again, he would dash into the midst of the enemy, cutting his way [with his saber] on the right hand and on the left, as if the strength of ten men lay in his single arm."

Daniel Horry, who commanded the South Carolinian cavalry, asked the wounded general for further orders. Pulaski answered, "Follow my lancers to whom I have given my orders for attack." The cavalrymen, however, devastated by the loss of their general, became dispirited and disorganized by the chaos of the battlefield.

Dr. James Lynah of Charleston quickly reached the bleeding Pulaski. With the help of Lynah's eighteen-year-old son, Edward, and a black servant named Guy, the doctor lifted and carried Pulaski still farther from the range of fire. Dr. Lynah operated immediately and removed the shell. Although the operation was extremely painful, Pulaski bore it with courage.

Had Pulaski remained in Dr. Lynah's care, he probably would have lived. However, Pulaski feared that if the British captured him, he might later be turned over to his hated enemy, the Russians. The Pole feared that the Russians would brag of his capture and then later execute him. Pulaski asked to be taken beyond the reach of the British. He endured agonizing pain as he was carried to the safety of an American ship, the *Wasp*. French surgeons came on board to drain the infected wound, but were unable to do so. Gangrene, the rapid decay of body tissues, set in. Pulaski suffered for five long days. On October 15, 1779, death alone conquered Count Casimir Pulaski.

Pulaski's body, dressed in his military uniform, was placed into a wooden coffin crafted by a member of the

Wasp's crew, a former Charleston cabinetmaker.

The coffin was transferred during the night from the ship to the plantation of Jane Bowen, who lived about 3 miles (4.8 km) from Savannah. In the presence of the Bowen family, Count Casimir Pulaski was buried in a torchlight service on the banks of the Wilmington River.

For a long time it was believed that Count Casimir Pulaski had died on board the Wasp on October 11, 1779, and was buried at sea.

However, in the 1960s, historian Edward Pinkowski discovered a letter written by Samuel Bulfinch, the captain of the Wasp, to General Benjamin Lincoln on October 15, 1779.

In his letter Bulfinch wrote, "I likewise took on board the Americans that were sent down, one of which died this day, and I have brought him ashore and buried him."

10. A Hero's Legacy

The French-American defeat at Savannah was a catastrophe. The French suffered 821 casualties and the Americans, 312 casualties. Well defended behind their fortifications, the British suffered minimal losses with 18 killed and 39 wounded. Only one British officer, a captain, was killed. By October 15, the Virginian and Georgian militias had left for home. Lincoln's army shrank to the remainder of Pulaski's Legion and two Continental regiments. Six days later the French forces and the ailing Admiral D'Estaing departed. Some ships sailed to France and some to the West Indies.

General Lincoln wrote to Congress on October 22 about the heavy losses suffered by the Southern army: "Our disappointment is great, and what adds much poignancy of our grief is the loss of a number of brave officers and men—among them the late intrepid Count Pulaski." The Congressional delegates rose up in praise of Pulaski. On November 22, 1779, a month after his death, they resolved to erect a monument in his honor.

Before the cornerstone to Pulaski's monument was set in 1853, the citizens of Savannah placed a number of items into a copper box within the cornerstone, including a silver dollar that had been found among the remains of soldiers who had died during the Siege of Savannah.

Without its dynamic commander, the Pulaski Legion rapidly fell apart. While fighting in South Carolina and Savannah, Pulaski had commanded a respectable cavalry corps composed of his legion and units of South Carolinian and Georgian cavalry. On November 14, 1780, Congress ordered that the remaining soldiers of the Pulaski Legion be added to the cavalry corps of Colonel Charles Armand.

Although the Pulaski Legion was disbanded, the American war in the South continued. In September 1781, Washington planned another combined French and American assault against the British general Charles Cornwallis in Yorktown, Virginia. After three days of battle, the British were trapped on land and by sea. Cornwallis officially surrendered to the Americans on October 19, 1781.

. . . .

The cornerstone of the Pulaski Monument in Savannah, Georgia, was laid on October 11, 1853. A cornerstone is a ceremonial part of a structure, often an engraved block. The ceremony's keynote speaker, Henry Williams, explained that the citizens of Savannah had gathered to honor "the gallant achievements and melancholy fate of that heroic son of Poland, that worshipper of Liberty and martyr in her cause, the friend and fellow-soldier of Washington, the noble and chivalrous Pulaski."

During his twenty-six months of service in the American Revolution, Pulaski made a lasting contribution to the American military. Pulaski's employment of the cavalry as an effective combat force would be recalled during the 1860s in the American Civil War, when the Confederate and Union armies routinely employed the powerful cavalry forces of Generals J.E.B. Stuart and Philip Sheridan.

Casimir Pulaski's lifelong struggle for freedom in Poland and America served as a beacon of hope for the Polish nation. The Polish people lost their freedom when Russia, Austria, and Prussia divided the country amongst themselves and wiped Poland off the map of Europe during the infamous partitions of 1772, 1793, and 1795. For 123 years, the ideals of Pulaski and his fellow freedom fighters such as Thaddeus Kosciuszko kept the Polish spirit alive. Finally, at the end of World War I in 1918, U.S. president Woodrow Wilson proclaimed the independence of Poland to be a required condition of the treaty of peace.

In honor of Casimir Pulaski's contributions to America, more than two hundred years later, there are many U.S. states that have a school, a street, a highway, a square, a county, or a town that is named for him. Though his life was short and tragic, Count Casimir Pulaski fulfilled his goal: To help America win its independence.

Timeline

1745	Count Casimir Pulaski is born in Warsaw, Poland, on March 6.
1760	Jozef Pulaski sends his fifteen-year-old son Casimir to stay at Prince Karl's court in Courland.
1768	Jozef Pulaski calls an organizational meeting in the remote town of Bar on February 29 to establish the Military Order of the Knights of the Holy Cross to resist the Russian occupation of Poland.
1768	Casimir Pulaski clashes with the Russian army on April 20 near the town of Staro-Konstantynow. He defends the town when more than four thousand Russian soldiers attack it four days later. Pulaski and his men manage to repel the Russian attacks for three days.
1771	Plotters kidnap King Stanislaw II August Poniatowski from his carriage in Warsaw on November 3. They abandon their plan. Pulaski is blamed for the attempt.
1773	Pulaski moves to Paris in March.
1777	Casimir Pulaski receives an official May 29 letter of recommendation addressed to George Washington from Benjamin Franklin in Paris.
	Casimir Pulaski lands in America on July 23 at Marblehead near Boston, Massachusetts.
	On August 28, General Washington asks Congress to appoint Pulaski to command the American cavalry.
	Count Pulaski takes part in the September 11 battle at Brandywine Creek.
	On September 15, Congress appoints Count Casimir Pulaski commander of the horse.

1778   Pulaski moves with his unit on January 9 to Trenton, New Jersey, where he organizes and trains the troops.

On March 1, Pulaski and his small cavalry unit defeat the superior British force in a surprise night attack at Haddonfield, New Jersey.

Pulaski receives Congressional permission to create an independent corps of cavalry and infantry on March 28.

A member of the Legion betrays Pulaski at Little Egg Harbor, New Jersey, on October 15. The Continental forces are surprised by the British in a night attack and suffer serious losses.

Pulaski's Legion is stationed in Minisink, New York, to guard frontier settlements in November.

1779   On February 2, Congress orders the Pulaski Legion to march to South Carolina.

Pulaski defends Charleston, South Carolina, on May 11.

The Pulaski Legion arrives at Savannah on September 14 to take part in the combined American and French attack against the British.

On October 9, Pulaski is mortally wounded in the attack on Savannah.

Pulaski dies on board the *Wasp* on October 15, while the ship is still anchored near Savannah. His body is taken to nearby Greenwich Plantation and buried there in a torchlight ceremony.

Glossary

Anglicized (ANG-glih-syzd) Changed a word to English usage.

animosity (a-neh-MAH-seh-tee) Feelings of hostility or hatred.

artillery (ar-TIH-lur-ee) Cannons, or other weapons for firing missiles.

autonomy (ah-TAH-nuh-mee) The state of being self-governing.

baptizing (BAP-tyz-ing) Sprinkling someone with or immersing someone in water to show that person's acceptance into the Christian faith.

bombard (bom-BARD) To attack with artillery.

ceded (SEED-ed) Yielded or granted, typically by treaty.

contrivances (kun-TRY-vents-ez) Something that has been created artificially.

disbanded (dis-BAND-ed) Broken up.

dispatched (dih-SPACHT) Sent with speed.

dragoons (druh-GOONZ) Heavily armed cavalry, sometimes described as mounted infantry.

encroaching (en-KROHCH-ing) Gradually intruding into the territory, possessions, or rights of another.

engulfed (in-GULFD) Overwhelmed.

exploits (EK-sployts) Adventures.

fervor (FER-ver) An intensity of emotion or passion.

flanking (FLANK-ing) Attacking the right or left side of a fort or a line of soldiers.

fortified (FOR-tuh-fyd) Defended against possible attack.

ingrates (IN-grayts) Ungrateful people.

initiative (ih-NIH-shuh-tiv) The first step in doing something.

interceded (in-ter-SEED-ed) To have helped two parties resolve their differences.

intrepid (in-TREH-pid) Fearless and bold.

maneuver (muh-NOO-ver) A military movement.

militia (muh-LIH-shuh) A group of volunteer or citizen soldiers who are organized to assemble in emergencies.

mortars (MOR-turz) Short-barrelled cannons used to send explosives high into the air.

oppression (uh-PREH-shun) The unjust use of power over another.

parish (PAR-ish) A church community.

precipitately (prih-SIH-pih-tet-lee) Showing undue haste.

rapport (ra-POR) A relationship marked by agreement and harmony.

rations (RA-shunz) A portion of food that is given out each day.

rebuffed (rih-BUFD) To have halted the progress or drive back the advance of another.

regicide (REH-jih-syd) The killing of a king, or a person who kills or helps to kill a king.

rudiments (ROO-dih-ments) Fundamental or basic skills.

siege (SEEJ) Blocking off a fort or a city with soldiers so that nothing can get in or go out.

squadron (SKWAH-drun) A cavalry unit made up of two or more groups.

tactics (TAK-tiks) Maneuvering forces into the best position before and during a battle.

tar-and-feathering (TAR-AND-FEH-thur-ing) Having to do with punishing a person by smearing him or her with tar and then covering him or her with feathers.

thwart (THWORT) To oppose or block the hopes or goals of another.

vexatious (vek-SAY-shus) Something that is annoying or bothersome.

volley (VAH-lee) Firing a number of weapons at the same time.

Additional Resources

To learn more about Casimir Pulaski and the American Revolution, check out these books and Web sites:

Books

Ambrus, Victor G. *Horses in Battle.* London: Oxford University Press, 1975.

Madison, Arnold. *Polish Greats.* New York: David McKay Company, Inc., 1980.

Web Sites

Due to the changing nature of Internet links, PowerPlus Books has developed an online list of Web sites related to the subject of this book. This site is updated regularly. Please use this link to access the list:
www.powerkidslinks.com/lalt/pulaski/

Bibliography

Ambrus, Victor G. *Horses in Battle*. London: Oxford University Press, 1975.

Carrington, Henry B. *Battles of the American Revolution, 1775–1781*. New York: A. S. Barnes & Company, 1888.

Chodzko, Leonard. *Zywot Kazimierza na Pulaziu Pulaskiego* [Life of Casimir on the Pulaski Estate]. Lwow: Poland, 1869.

"Count Pulaski of Poland." In *The Papers of Benjamin Franklin*. Edited by William B. Willcox. Vol. 24. New Haven: Yale University Press, 1982.

George Washington Papers, 1741–1799. "Pulaski to Washington," December 19 and December 29, 1777, MF Series 4, Reel 46. Washington D.C., National Archives.

Gordon, William R. "Count Casimir Pulaski." *Georgia Historical Quarterly* 13, no. 3 (October 1929): 169–227.

Kajencki, Francis Casimir. *Casimir Pulaski: Cavalry Commander of the American Revolution*. Reprint, El Paso, TX: Southwest Polonia Press, 2002.

Konopczynski, Wladyslaw. *Casimir Pulaski*. Chicago: Polish Roman Catholic Union of America, 1947.

Lewis, John Frederick, President of the Historical Society of Pennsylvania. "An Address Delivered in Independence Square: October 12, 1929." *The Pennsylvania Magazine of History and Biography* 55, no. 1 (1931).

Lossing, Benson J. *Pictorial Field-Book of the Revolution*. 2 vols. New York: Harper, 1851–52.

Lukowski, Jerzy and Hubert Zawadzki. *A Concise History of Poland*. Cambridge, United Kingdom: Cambridge University Press, 2001.

Manning, Clarence A. *Soldier of Liberty, Casimir Pulaski*. New York: Philosophical Library, 1945.

Mattern, David B. *Benjamin Lincoln and the American Revolution.* Columbia: University of South Carolina Press, 1995.

Pinkowski Institute, Cooper City, Florida. http://www.poles.org/birth.html.

Pulaski, Francois, ed. *Correspondance du General Casimir Pulaski avec Claude de Rulhiere, 1774–1778.* Paris: Societe Historique et Litteraire Polanaise, 1948, Library of Congress.

Ramsay, David. *The History of the American Revolution, 1785.* Edited by Lester H. Cohen. Reprinted 1990. 2 vols. Indianapolis: Liberty Fund, Inc., 1990.

Randall, Willard Sterne. *George Washington: A Life.* New York: Henry Holt, 1997.

Sparks, Jared. "Count Pulaski, A Memoir." The Library of American Biography. Vol. 14. Boston: Charles R. Little and James Brown, 1845.

Szymanski, Leszek. *Casimir Pulaski: A Hero of the American Revolution.* New York: Hippocrene Books, Inc., 1993.

Waniczek, Helena. "Casimir Pulaski: 'Father of American Cavalry' 1747–79." *Great Men and Women of Poland.* Ed. Stephen P. Mizwa. New York: Macmillan, 1941.

Wood, W. J. *Battles of the Revolutionary War: 1775–1781.* New York: Da Capo Press, 1995.

Index

About the Author

Since 1990, Dr. AnnMarie Francis Kajencki has been an editorial consultant for Southwest Polonia Press. In this role she has critically reviewed the firm's manuscripts, primarily relating to American history, for publication. The doctor has written this children's book based on her father's book, *Casimir Pulaski: Cavalry Commander of the American Revolution*. Dr. Kajencki is also a professor of English at Bismarck State College in Bismarck, North Dakota. She regularly writes presentations for national and regional conferences on English and education. She lives on the mighty Missouri River in a house she shares with five cats.

About the Consultant

Francis Casimir Kajencki was born in Erie, Pennsylvania, in 1918. He entered the United States Military Academy, at West Point, New York, in 1939. In 1973, after thirty years of commissioned service, he retired as assistant chief of information, Department of the Army. Colonel Kajencki began researching military history, and wrote several books on American history. His latest book is *Casimir Pulaski: Cavalry Commander of the American Revolution*. Colonel Kajencki resides in El Paso, Texas.

Primary Sources

Cover. *Casimir Pulaski*, oil painting, ca. 1897, Julian Rys, Independence National Historical Park; Background, *Kazimierz Pulawski at the Battle of Czestochowa, December 1770*, watercolor, 1883, Juliusz Fortunat Kossak, Private Collection/Bridgeman Art Library. **Page 4.** *See cover.* **Page 7.** Enlistment poster for Polish army, lithograph, 1917, W. T. Benda, Library of Congress Prints and Photographs Division. **Page 10.** *View of Krakowskie Przedmiescie from Ulica Nowy Swiat, Warsaw, 1778*, oil painting, Bernardo Bellotto, courtesy of Lauros/Giraudon/Bridgeman Art Library. **Page 12.** *The Election of the King Stanislaus Augustus*, oil painting, Bernardo Bellotto, Royal Castle, Warsaw, Poland/Bridgeman Art Library. **Page 13.** *Catherine II of Russia*, oil painting, ca. 1700s, French school, courtesy of Chateau de Versailles, France/Bridgeman Art Library. **Page 19.** *See cover.* **Page 23.** *Charles James Fox addressing the House of Commons during the Pitt Ministry*, oil painting, ca. 1766–1768, Anton Hickel, Houses of Parliament, Westminster, London, UK/Bridgeman Art Library. **Page 24.** Guidelines for the Stamp Act, publication, 1766, printed by Mark Baskett, courtesy of Manuscript Division, Library of Congress. **Page 25.** *The Repeal or Funeral of Miss Anne-Stamp*, cartoon, published in 1766, Library of Congress Prints and Photographs Division. **Page 27.** Glass bottle with tea leaves from the Boston Tea Party, 1773, collected by T. M. Harris, Massachusetts Historical Society, Boston, MA, USA/Bridgeman Art Library. **Page 30.** *General Howe Evacuating Boston*, oil painting, 1861, John Godfrey and Michael A. Wageman II, Collections of the New York Public Library, Astor, Lenox, and Tilden Foundations. **Page 31.** *L'Entré triumphale de troupes royales a Nouvelle Yorck*, engraving, ca. 1770s, Francis Xavier Habermann, Prints and Photographs Division, Library of Congress. **Page 32.** *Washington Crossing the Delaware*, oil painting, ca. 1856, George Caleb Bingham, courtesy of Chrysler Museum of Art, gift of Walter P. Chrysler Jr. **Page 36.** A letter from Benjamin Franklin to George Washington, May 29, 1777, George Washington Papers at the Library of Congress, 1741–1799, Series 4, Library of Congress, Rare Book and Special Collections Division. **Page 39.** *Tadeusz Kosciuszko*, lithograph, 1917, George Illian, Prints and Photographs Division, Library of Congress. **Page 40.** *Battle of the Brandywine*, engraving, 1898, Frederick Coffay Yohn, Northwind Picture Archive. **Page 43.** Journals of the Continental Congress from September 15, 1777, National Archives and Records Administration, Old Military and Civil Records. **Page 46.** *George Washington Taking the Salute at Trenton*, oil painting, ca. 1899, John Faed, The Warner Collection of Gulf States Paper Corporation, Tuscaloosa, Alabama. **Page 48–49.** *Die helden der revolution*, engraving, ca. 1850–1890, Frederick Girsch, Prints and Photographs Division, Library of Congress. **Page 50.** *John Laurens*, oil painting, ca. 1784, Charles Willson Peale, courtesy of Independence National Historic Park. **Page 56.** *The Manege Gallop with the Right Leg* (top) and *Terre a Terre to the Right* (bottom), oil paintings, ca.1750, Thomas Butler, who based his work on drawings by John Vanderbank that were published by Josephus Sympson in the 1729 *25 Actions of the Manage Horse*, Gavin Graham Gallery, London, UK, Private Collection/Bridgeman Art Library. **Page 58.** Officers' pistols (*top*) and American Horseman Saber (*bottom*), ca. 1700s and 1773–1783, respectively, courtesy of the George C. Neumann Collection, Valley Forge National Historical Park. **Page 61.** A letter from Count Casimir Pulaski to George Washington, February 28, 1778, George Washington Papers at the Library of Congress, 1741–1799, Series 4, Library of Congress, Rare Book and Special Collections Division. **Page 65.** A letter from George Washington to Count Casimir Pulaski, March 3, 1778, George Washington Papers at the Library of Congress, 1741–1799, Series 4, Library of Congress, Rare Book and Special Collections Division. **Page 73.** *Back of the State House*, Plate 22 of *Birch's Views of Philadelphia*, engraving, ca. 1798, William Birch, courtesy of Independence National Historic Park. **Page 75.** An excerpt from a map of the Province of New Jersey, 1778, engraved and published by William Faden, Library of Congress Geography and Map Division. **Page 76.** *Soldier of the Hessen-Hanau Regiment Erbprinz*, watercolor, late 1800s, E. Sack, based on an earlier work by Captain Friedrich von Germann, Print Collection, Miriam and Ira D. Wallach Division of Art, Prints, and Photographs, New York Public Library, Astor, Lenox, and Tilden Foundations. **Page 79.** An accounting of the men and horses in Count Casimir Pulaski's regiment of light horse, 1779, printed by John Dunlap, Chicago Historical Society. **Page 81.** *Augustin Prevost*, oil painting, ca. 1800s, Mather Brown, Private Collection/Bridgeman Art Library. **Page 83.** *John Rutledge*, oil painting, ca. 1888, Robert Hinckley, based on an earlier ca. 1791 work by John Trumbull, U.S. Supreme Court Historical Society. **Page 84.** *An Exact Prospect of Charlestown: the Metropolis of the Province of South Carolina*, first published in a London magazine in 1762, Library of Congress Geography and Map Division. **Page 87.** *Count D'Estaing*, 1769, oil painting, Jean Baptiste Lebrun, Chateau de Versailles, France/Bridgeman Art Library. **Page 89.** A Map of the Siege of Savannah, 1779, Pierre Ozanne, Library of Congress Geography and Map Division.

Credits

Photo Credits

Cover (portrait), p.4, 50, 73 Courtesy Independence National Historical Park; cover (background), pp.19, 81 Private Collection/Bridgeman Art Library; pp. 7, 24, 25, 28, 31, 36, 39, 48-49, 61, 65, 75, 84, 89 Library of Congress; p. 9 courtesy of Edward Pinkowski, the Pinkowski Institute; p. 10 Muzeum Narodowe, Warsaw, Poland/Bridgeman Art Library; p. 12 Royal Castle, Warsaw, Poland/Bridgeman Art Library; p. 13 Chateau de Versailles, France/Bridgeman Art Library; pp. 14, 15 Anne S.K. Brown Military Collection, Brown University Library; p. 16 National Museum in Cracow, Poland/Bridgeman Art Library; p. 23 Houses of Parliament, Westminster, London, UK/Bridgeman Art Library; p. 27 Massachusetts Historical Society, Boston, MA, USA/Bridgeman Art Library; p. 30 Collections of the New York Public Library, Astor, Lenox, and Tilden Foundations; p. 32 Chrysler Museum of Art, gift of Walter P. Chrysler Jr. in honor of Walter P. Chrysler Sr.; p. 35 Maura B. McConnell; p. 40 © North Wind Picture Archives; p. 43 NARA; p. 46 The Warner Collection of Gulf States Paper Corporation, Tuscaloosa, Alabama; p. 53 Military Image Bank; p. 55 © Ted Spiegel/CORBIS; p. 56 Private Collection/Bridgeman Art Library; p. 58 George C. Neumann Collection, Valley Forge National Historical Park, photos by Cindy Reiman; p. 68 Maryland Historical Society; p. 69 courtesy of the Hotel Bethlehem, Bethlehem, PA; p. 70 © Hulton/Archive/Getty Images; p. 76 Print Collection, Miriam and Ira D. Wallach Division of Art, Prints, and Photographs, New York Public Library Astor, Lenox, and Tilden Foundations; p. 79 Chicago Historical Society; p. 83 U.S. Supreme Court Historical Society; p. 87 Chateau de Versailles, France/Bridgeman Art Library; p. 93 Polish Museum of America, Chicago; p. 97 Georgia Historical Society.

Project Editor Daryl Heller

Series Design Laura Murawski

Layout Design Maria Melendez, Ginny Chu
Kim Sonsky

Photo Researcher Jeffrey Wendt